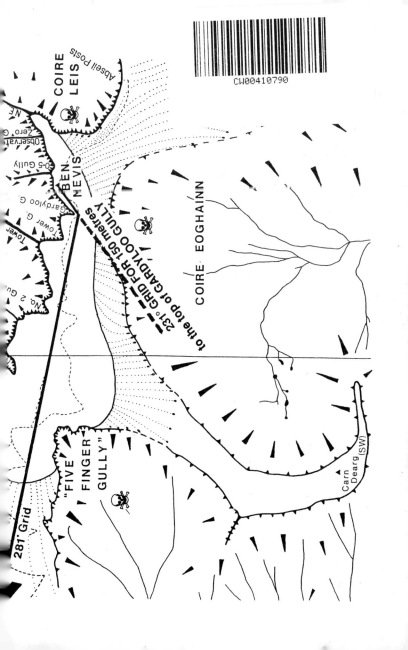

WINTER CLIMBS
BEN NEVIS AND GLENCOE

Looking across from Zero Gully to climbers entering the 'Basin' on Orion Face Direct.

WINTER CLIMBS
BEN NEVIS AND GLENCOE

BY

ALAN KIMBER

Diagrams by R.B.Evans
(except where stated)

CICERONE PRESS
MILNTHORPE, CUMBRIA

ISBN 1 85284 072 2

First Edition (by I.S.Clough) March 1969
Second Edition (Revised by H.MacInnes) March 1974
Third Edition (by Ed Grindley) February 1981
Fourth Edition (by Alan Kimber) February 1991

Front Cover: On Curved Ridge, Buachaille Etive Mor.
Climber: Lindsay McKenzie. Photo: Alan Kimber

Back Cover: Gardyloo Buttress - Smith's Route (V).
Climber: Lindsay Griffin. Photo: Alan Kimber

CONTENTS

PREFACE & ACKNOWLEDGEMENTS

This new edition of *Winter Climbs - Ben Nevis and Glencoe,* has many new routes, some new areas, more information and some up-dated illustrations. Whilst compiling the details I have had considerable help from a wide range of climbers who have been kind enough to give time and thought to my questions. My thanks go the the following people: Rab Anderson; Nick Banks; 'Tut' Braithwaite; Brian Chambers; Robin Clothier; Ken Crocket; Dave 'Cubby' Cuthbertson; Chris Dale; Mal Duff; Davy Gardiner; Alex Gillespie; Ed Grindley; Con Higgins; Geoff Hornby; Arthur Paul; Simon Richardson; Klaus Schwartz; Colin Stead and the SMC for allowing considerable use to be made of their 'Journal'; Chris Smaje; Noel Williams; Roger Wild; Blyth Wright and the Scottish Avalanche Service. Sorry if I have missed anyone!!

In the process of talking to climbers about the routes outlined in this edition it has been interesting to note how many have disagreed on route detail, especially with some of the harder climbs. It is in the nature of the game that we play which is dictated by 'conditions' which cause some variance to the original line. Winter guidebook details will always be much harder to follow than the summer rock climb with its clinical breakdown of moves and rock features. Such is the mystery and uncertainty of an ice/snow covered mountain. Hopefully this guide will lead climbers to the foot of the route and help them assess a way to the top. In between much will be left up to their experience and ability to handle different conditions en route.

In the final analysis the guidebook author must take the blame for incorrect or poor detail and obvious omissions. Please contact me with your criticisms or praise if it is felt necessary. Only by continuing feedback from the guidebook users will this guidebook to Britain's most important winter climbing area progress.

Good climbing,

Alan Kimber
Mountain guide and guidebook author,
15 Annat View, Corpach, Fort William.

Gardyloo Gully in October. The wall and tunnel behind the climber is often completely obliterated later in the winter. On this occasion the route was grade III.

INTRODUCTION

Ben Nevis; the peaks of Glencoe and the surrounding mountains give some of the best snow and ice climbing anywhere in Europe, when the conditions are right. So popular and well known is Ben Nevis, that in recent years climbers from as far afield as Poland, Australia, France, Italy and the USA have been seen trudging the delights of the 'famous' Allt a'Mhuilinn approach. Hamish MacInnes and Yvon Chouinard have made films of winter climbing on Ben Nevis, as have French guides, who continue to bring clients back each year. Justifiably a good 'tick' on any discerning world travellers' itinerary.

Budding mountaineers and climbers from the British Isles are fortunate in having these peaks so close, as they provide excellent training for people intending to visit the Alps or greater ranges of the world, whether climbing or trekking. Today's winter specialists will find more than enough climbing to the highest of modern technical standards to encourage them back, year after year.

Many of the routes are longer than experienced anywhere else in British hills and of alpine-like seriousness. It is not a good idea to be lured onto the famous 'Tower Ridge' of Ben Nevis as your first Scottish winter climb. The lads from the Lochaber Mountain Rescue Team have escorted dozens of shivering 'all nighters' off this route in the dull grey hours of dawn!! Try something shorter to start with as a 'Wee Scottish Apprenticeship'.

A combination of short daylight hours and possible strong winds, poor weather and snow conditions add to the serious nature of Scottish climbing. Fitness is of prime importance to sustain climbers through long hours, carrying far more weight in the rucksacks than would be experienced in the summer months. Climbers must be economical with their time and aim to keep moving as fluently as is practical, in order to avoid a possibly serious 'benightment' or slip on a dark unknown descent. Records show that novice and experienced climbers alike come to grief on these Scottish mountains, sometimes with fatal consequences.

The winter season varies greatly. Generally the best months will be February, March and April, with some excellent conditions often appearing in April high on Ben Nevis, but not on the lower surrounding peaks. The first winter snows arrive in September, but often are short-lived in the moist Atlantic airstream. October and certainly November can provide good but lean climbing conditions early on. However, these months, along with the Christmas and New year period are something of a lottery, with short daylight hours. The easier grade one gullies can often be climbed right through to June/July, especially on Ben Nevis where large patches of snow remain in the shadowy hollows all year round. Point Five Gully has been climbed as early as November and as late as May.

In compiling this guidebook for winter climbers visiting Ben Nevis and Glencoe, the author, Alan Kimber has drawn on twenty years of experience gained from living in Fort William. During that period he has worked as both instructor and mountain guide with a variety of different organisations from private outdoor centres to national bodies for mountain training. Alongside this day to day work a deep sense of personal satisfaction and enjoyment has been gained from travelling and climbing amongst Britain's highest and most demanding peaks in winter.

As well as a deep understanding of the peaks in this guidebook, the author has gained from visits to the Himalayas, Peru, Alaska, Baffin Island, Labrador and Africa, plus numerous seasons in the European Alps. At present he runs his own mountain training and guiding company based in Corpach, a small village four miles outside Fort William.

WEATHER AND AVALANCHES

The area covered by this guidebook is well known as having some of the most severe weather in the British Isles. A combination of strong winds and snowfall coupled with fluctuating temperatures provide the climber with potential life-threatening situations of a varied nature. Before setting out on any climb it is wise for climbers to inform themselves of the likely snow and weather conditions they are likely to meet.

In response to the steadily increasing number of avalanche incidents the Scottish Mountain Safety Group has appointed three teams of Observers, one in the Cairngorms, one in Glencoe and one in

Lochaber (1990).

These teams of experienced mountaineers monitor and report on snow conditions and avalanche risk on a daily basis throughout the winter. (A report is also issued for Lochnagar once a week to cover weekends. Comparative studies of snowpack structure should increase our understanding of the nature and cause of avalanches in these popular mountain areas.

A snow conditions and avalanche report is prepared each day and made available to the public through the national media as well as local outlets. Through these reports it is hoped to provide the climber, walker and off-piste skier with up to date, reliable information on snow conditions, avalanche danger and the effect of weather on these. This will aid the mountain user in making decisions regarding route choice in planning a safe and enjoyable excursion into the hills.

It cannot be stated too strongly that even the most sophisticated forecast is only an adjunct to the range of information available to the mountaineer. It is not a substitute for good judgement but rather an aid to better judgement.

Snow and Avalanche Reports

Reports are prepared every day and are available from:

MOUNTAIN CALL	East: 0898 500 442
	West: 0898 500 441
CLIMB LINE	East Highlands: 0898 654 668
	West Highlands: 0898 654 669

Radio and television news bulletins, notice-boards and other strategic locations in the Glencoe, Cairngorm and Lochaber and Lochnagar areas.

Avalanche Awareness
BEFORE SETTING OUT

1. Seek expert local advice. Avalanches can have certain characteristics which are peculiar to one area. Even experienced mountaineers can benefit from local knowledge.

2. Get the most recent snow and avalanche report and weather forecast.

3. Find out about the weather during the past week. How has this

affected snow conditions? Will the forecast weather increase or decrease the risk of avalanches?

4. Be prepared to modify your plans in the light of this information.

ON ROUTE

5. The most reliable indicator of avalanche danger is signs of recent avalanche activity. Is this confined to slopes of a particular orientation?

6. Observe the condition of the snow as you go along:
   Is there evidence of drifting?
   Wind Slab is the most common type of avalanche!
   How deep is the new snow?
   The deeper the snow, the greater the stress and therefore the danger.
   Is it getting warmer or colder?
   A sudden change in temperature is a common trigger.
   Cold weather prolongs avalanche risk.
   A rapid thaw of unconsolidated snow causes wet avalanches.

7. Have a close look at the surface layer of snow where the majority of avalanches occur. Use your axe or ski to dig through this layer to the one below. How firmly does the surface layer adhere to the one below? If it breaks away easily then all slopes of similar aspect and altitude should be avoided.

8. Follow a line which avoids suspect slopes and the possibility of being swept onto rocks should a slide occur.

If You Witness an Avalanche

- OBSERVE the victim's progress and mark both the starting point and the point at which last seen.
- CHECK for further avalanche danger.
- Make a THOROUGH SEARCH of the debris surface:
  - LOOK for any sign of victims
  - LISTEN for any sounds
  - SEARCH the most likely burial spots
- Make a SYSTEMATIC SEARCH, probing the debris with axes or ski poles with baskets removed.

- If a victim is recovered, administer FIRST AID.
- Send someone for help.

If You are Caught in an Avalanche

* An initial loud shout may help in letting others know of your problem. Do not continue to shout too much as snow entering the lungs can cause serious damage. In fact it is a good idea to keep your mouth shut most of the time.

* Try and delay your slide by digging into the underlying base on which the avalanche is sliding. This is only practical if the avalanche is a shallow one. Also it may be possible to hold onto rocks or trees.

* Try and keep your head uphill and stay on your back with arms outstretched in a wide backstroke swimming motion.

* Jettison your rucksack, as it can pull you down into the snowpack.

* A final supreme effort as the avalanche slows will hopefully bring you to the surface or create an airspace.

* Good luck!!!

Recommended Reading
A Chance in a Million by Barton and Wright, pub. Scottish Mountaineering Trust.
Mountaincraft and Leadership by Langmuir, pub. Scottish Sports Council and Mountain-Walking Leadership Training Board.

Using the Snow and Avalanche Report
LOOK AT:

* Date and time of issue - the Report is valid at this time. Conditions may change very rapidly.

* Avalanche risk - states the risk on scale Very Low to Very High and also on numeric scale 1-5 (see below). Includes general statement, noting highest risk areas and details of avalanches actually observed.

* Avalanche outlook for the day following day of issue. This will be correct IF THE WEATHER OUTLOOK IS CORRECT. If the weather outlook is inaccurate, you must use you own judgement to assess the effect on avalanche risk.

THE 5 POINT SCALE

Category 1 (Very Low) - Usually applies in conditions where rock-hard nevé exists, with no new snowfall or drifting. Slow thaw of old snow could also produce this nearly zero-risk situation.

Category 2 (Low) - Generally stable snowpack, with minimum risk of large avalanches. Any new snow is stable; old snow either hard frozen or if thawing, unlikely to produce wet slides.

Category 3 (Medium) - Accumulations of new snow or slab are unlikely to be as great as 30cm and generally are stable, although localised avalanches are possible. In thaw conditions, wet sluffs are possible, but larger slabs unlikely. Occasional spontaneous avalanching possible.

Category 4 (High) - High risk of victim-triggered avalanche of any type, with the possibility of large avalanches. Some spontaneous avalanching likely.

Category 5 (Very High) - Extreme risk of spontaneous avalanches of any kind, including the largest wet or dry slabs.

Note: CORNICES. Cornice collapse is possible at Category 3 (Medium) and upwards. As well as being a danger in itself, this is a common trigger for avalanche.

Thanks to Blyth Wright and Scottish Avalanche Service for supplying information relating to avalanche assessment.

EQUIPMENT AND SAFETY PRECAUTIONS

Map and Compass

This guidebook will hopefully help climbers to find their route. It must be used in conjunction with a weatherproof map. All the areas in this guide are covered by the:

O.S. Landranger series, Sheet 41, Ben Nevis, Fort William and surrounding area, 1:50,000

Ben Nevis, The Aonachs and Stob Ban are also covered on the O.S. Outdoor Leisure 32, Mountainmaster, Ben Nevis, the Grey Corries and the Mamores, 1:25,000 map.

The ability to use these maps with a compass is of prime importance to all winter mountaineers and climbers.

Ice Axe/Hammer/Crampons

Ice axe and crampons are essential for any winter outing, whether walking or climbing. For climbing it is assumed that two tools (axe and hammer) are used, either drooped pick or inclined (banana) model. Many good tools are available and the first-time buyer might consider a modular system which allows new picks to be fitted at a reduced cost when compared to buying a complete axe/hammer. Tools should be 50/55cm in length for climbing.

Boots

Stiff plastic boots with well maintained vibram sole are best for winter climbing and when linked to a pair of clip-on crampons provide a solid and positive base for the necessary footwork involved in climbing snow and ice.

Helmet

A climbing helmet is recommended, especially when climbing below other parties who may be dislodging large brick-sized lumps of ice from above.

Climbing Protection

For protection on steep ground, rock pegs should be carried along with the full array of more modern chocks and equipment. Be aware though that too much gear weighs you down and slows the day. Only take what is required for the route, e.g. Tower Ridge does not require ice screws or dead-men, whilst Point Five will. I well remember seeing a party of climbers in Gardyloo Gully (Grade 1 at the time) festooned with every gadget available, from 'Friends' to 'Wallnuts'. The nearest rock was buried under three metres of snow and they did not have a dead-man with them. A 45m or 50m rope is recommended.

Body Comforts

Food and spare clothing should be carried - light thermal layers are far better than chunky sweaters and duvets. Try and keep the weight to a minimum. A sensible balance between lightness and safety is required. A bivvy bag should be considered as it will certainly come in handy one day along with a headtorch and spare battery and bulb.

NOTES ON THE USE OF THIS GUIDE

Gradings

Much debate has taken place over the years concerning the grading of Scottish winter climbs. It continues to bubble and boil and will no doubt still be without a solid foundation when the next guidebook is published! The status quo has been maintained for this edition and the grade of I-VI used, as in the previous guide by Ed Grindley. Changes to the grades of climbs which appeared in that guide may have been made if the original ascentionists or public opinion has asked for a change.

The following grades are for average conditions and it should be remembered that winter climbs can vary enormously from time to time, depending on snow or ice build-up and the weather. Early in the season when conditions can be lean, certain routes will be harder than later on when a good plating of ice covers blank stretches, making them easier. Also it must be remembered that the passage of a mild weather system over the whole of the area covered by this guide will change the character and difficulty of many climbs overnight.

Grade I   Straightforward snow climbs containing no ice pitches. Large cornices may exist, especially on Ben Nevis and the Aonachs.

Grade II   These gullies contain minor ice pitches, may have high angled snow and difficult cornice exits. The easier buttresses which under winter cover provide more continuous difficulty.

Grade III Less straightforward climbs than the previous grades would suggest. This grade can contain long stretches of ice and snow to a high angle as well as prolonged difficulties on rocky ridges. A grade which should only be attempted by experienced parties.

Grade IV   Covers a wide variety of routes ranging from almost vertical ice and rock on some of the shorter routes to less steep but very sustained climbs.

Grade V   Everything that is Grade IV but much more of it. Serious climbs of great length which include long steep sections

Brenva Face, Moonwalk (III/IV) Climber: Klaus Schwartz

First ascent of Gemini, Direct Start (V)
Climber: Alex McIntyre   Photo: Alan Kimber
First pitch of Point Five Gully (V)
Climber: George Grassam   Photo: Alan Kimber

and possibly serious and poorly protected long run-outs.

Grade VI What can possibly be harder than Grade V? The answer is definitely a great deal!! Especially if something like Point Five is taken as a standard Grade V gully and Orion direct a standard Grade V face climb under good conditions. This grade includes movement on blank, steep sparsely iced up cliffs using ice tools jammed in cracks (torqueing) and crampons sparking on bare rock or very thin ice. It could also include routes like Point Five and Zero in very poor thin conditions!

N.B. A split grade such as III/IV indicates the possibility of a wide variation in difficulties depending on conditions.

Timing

Times are dispensed with in this edition. Climbers should start early and be capable of assessing their ability to 'top out' before dark. All the climbs in this guide can be climbed in a day but a headtorch is recommended just in case.

Length of Climb

Length of climbs and where possible pitch lengths are given in metres. Route lengths are as accurate as possible and will hopefully give the climber at least a reasonable idea of the scale of the route.

Recommended Routes

Where possible a three star system has been used to indicate quality under good conditions, the more stars the better the route. However, many routes under good conditions would warrant some special mention. This star system will hopefully allow the stranger to the area to find some good climbing on their first visit.

RESCUE FACILITIES

The Mountain Rescue teams of Lochaber and Glencoe (civilian volunteers) attend more call-outs than all the other Scottish teams put together. Along with the RAF (helicopter and land-based teams) they provide an excellent service. They are very experienced and skillful local mountaineers. Rescues are co-ordinated by the Police, who should be contacted on 999 in case of an accident or possible problem. DO NOT DELAY IN RAISING THE ALARM IF YOU FEEL SOMEBODY IS IN NEED OF HELP.

Public Telephones and M.R. Posts

Ben Nevis	Youth Hostel in Glen Nevis (GR 127717)
	Distillery (GR 125757)
	Golf Course Club House (GR 136762)
Glencoe	Kingshouse Hotel (M.R. Post - GR 259546)
	Achnambeithach (M.R. Post - GR 140565)
	Clachaig Hotel (GR 128567)

For climbers on Ben Nevis a direct radio link with the Police in Fort William is situated in the small annexe on the left, outside the main entrance to the C.I.C. Hut. Open the door and lift up the large wooden flap in front of you. This will reveal a simple handset. Push the button (white in 1990) and keep it depressed whilst asking for the Police. The following will be sufficient: ... Fort William Police ... Fort William Police ... this is C.I.C. Hut ... C.I.C. Hut ... Can you hear me? ... Release the white button and wait for the Police to reply. Give your message (don't forget to push the white button every time you speak and release it every time you want to listen. Should you get no reply at first, keep trying. If after several attempts you still get no reply, give your message anyway. Be clear and economical with what you say. Give brief details of where the accident has taken place (name the route), the nature of any injuries if known and how many people are involved. Stay by the radio until the rescue team arrives.

On Ben Nevis at present three emergency shelters exist: Coire Leis - GR 173713; Carn Dearg NW - GR 158719: and on the summit of Ben Nevis.

Of these three very small shelters the only one that is of any use as a shelter against the elements in winter is on Ben Nevis summit itself. The other two structures are very often buried under many feet of snow and filled full of spin-drift early in the winter. Do not rely on finding them and then spending much time and effort excavating them. That time and effort could easily be used to get off the hill.

AMENITIES

Fort William and Glencoe are well supplied with all the necessary facilities required by climbers.

Transport

Coaches travel daily from Glasgow, passing through Glencoe en route. Trains arrive at Fort William daily and it is not unknown for climbers from London to catch the sleeper on a Friday evening, climb on Saturday and Sunday, then head back to work on the Sunday night train!

Glasgow or Inverness airports are both approximately two hours drive from Fort William.

Shops

Four specialist climbing shops can be found:
Glencoe Guides and Gear (GR 095586)
West Coast Outdoor Leisure, High Street, Fort William
Nevisport, High Street, Fort William
Brighams, (opposite the hospital).

Of particular interest to climbers coming down late are the Spar shops in Claggan (GR 117743) and Ballachulish (GR 083583), where all foodstuffs can be found to fill the hungriest belly. Mobile Chippies can be found lurking around various housing schemes in Fort William, Caol and Corpach. For the more discerning a visit to the Nevisport restaurant will empty your pocket and fill your stomach.

Cinema

Cameron Square, High Street, Fort William.

Hospital

The Belford Hospital (GR 106741).

Doctors

Fort William (0397) 703773/703136/702947
Glencoe (08552) 226.

Police Station
Fort William (0397) 702361
Glencoe (08552) 222.

**Climbing Wall and Swimming Pool
(GR 109742).**

Avalanche & Weather Information
Local Climbing Shops and Nevisbank Hotel.

Accommodation
This section is intended to offer advice on accommodation for the whole area.

Climbers visiting the area covered by this guide should have no problems with places to rest their weary heads! Everything from five-star hotels to flooded campsites are available.

The following is a small list of the selection available and reflects the style of accommodation which climbers generally appreciate (?)!

Kingshouse Hotel and Bunkhouse. Tel: Kingshouse (08556) 259

Glen Nevis Youth Hostel. Tel: Fort William (0397) 702336

Glencoe Youth Hostel. Tel: Ballachulish (08552) 219

Clachaig Hotel and Chalets. Tel: Ballachulish (08552) 252

McColl's Bunkhouse and Cottage. Tel: Ballachulish (08552) 256

Onich Inchree Chalets. Tel: Onich (08553) 287

Snowgoose Holidays (Bunkhouse). Tel: Corpach (0397) 772467

Bunkhouse Kinloch Leven. Tel: Kinlochleven (08554) 471.

Eight climbing huts are situated in the area from Crianlarich to Fort William. A complete list of these is available from the BMC in Manchester, Tel: (061) 2735835.

According to Ian Nicholson, (the first person to solo Point Five and Zero gullies before lunch, and who now runs the Kingshouse Hotel) free camping is available at this exposed spot ... "for the tough"!

For a complete list of all types of accommodation, from hotels to campsites contact the Fort William and Lochaber Tourist Office, Tel: (0397) 703781 and ask for their accommodation guide. A glance through the back pages of *Climber and Hillwalker* or *High* magazines will illuminate further possibilities.

Mountain Guides

For anyone wishing to hire the services of a member of the British Association of Mountain Guides in order to explore the climbs in this book in the company of a local expert, three local outfits offer a comprehensive service:

Alan Kimber (Professional Mountaineering Services)

Tel: (0397) 772726

Paul Moores (Glencoe Guides and Gear) Tel: (08552) 402

Mick Tighe (Nevis Guides) Tel: (039781) 356 or 513.

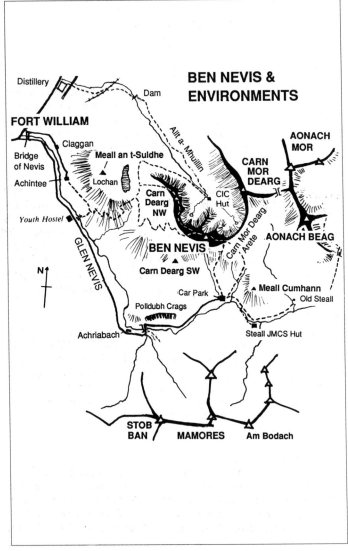

BEN NEVIS

APPROACHES FOR BEN NEVIS

Approaches for climbs on the N.E. aspect of Ben Nevis all aim initially for the C.I.C. Hut (GR 167722). This hut is private and bookings can be made through Bob Richardson, 2 Inch Lonaig Drive, Balloch, Glasgow, G83 8JH. (OS Map sheet 41 Ben Nevis 1:50,000 or OS Outdoor Leisure Map sheet 32 Mountain Master 1:25,000.

Distillery Approach
Parking is available near the telephone box (GR 124756). A donation to the local M.R. team can be made in return for this at the Distillery Office. The paths shown on the maps are accurate and lead in $1^{1}/_{2}$-2 hours to the hut. Initially it is necessary to walk through the premises of the distillery before crossing the railway line and linking into the path system that leads up the hill. On striking a good motorable track (private) follow it to the dam (GR 147751). From this dam the path follows the east bank of the Allt a'Mhuilinn (boggy) to the hut.

Golf Club Approach
A slightly shorter route. Please keep off the greens at all times. Parking is available in the Golf Club car park (GR 136762). Please respect the main users of this facility; the golfers! One positive aspect of using this approach is that the Golf Club Bar is often open on returning to the valley, especially if you are late down! Walk through the tunnel under the railway and cross the golf course and walk up the east side of the stream following a good path which links in with the first approach, $1^{1}/_{2}$- 2 hours.

Glen Nevis Approach
The approach from the south-west follows the zig-zag 'Pony Track' (Tourist Route to the summit) as far as the broad saddle between Meall an t-Suidhe and the main massif of Carn Dearg NW, Ben Nevis. This track starts from Achintee Farm (GR 125729). A popular alternative is to start from the Youth Hostel in Glen Nevis (GR 127717) and

climb steeply to join the main track. Access and parking is also available for the Pony Track route by the footbridge over the River Nevis (GR 123731).

Above the saddle which holds the large Lochan Meall an t-Suidhe (or 'Half-way Lochan Grid Square 1472) the pony track veers back to the right (south) crosses the Red Burn, and zig-zags up the long slope to the summit plateau. Where the pony track swings to the south, the route to the hut branches off northwards. It follows an indefinite path contouring the lower slopes of Carn Dearg above the Half-way Lochan for about one km until it reaches the remains of an old fence on the lip of the Allt a'Mhuilinn glen. From this point it gradually descends for about 30 metres in a north-easterly direction and then continues traversing south-east across the hillside until it reaches the Allt a'Mhuilinn (500 metres below the C.I.C. Hut). A large boulder, the Lunching Stone, will be seen on the left of the path along this traverse. The route now follows the right bank of the Allt a'Mhuilinn burn until it is joined by another large stream coming in from the right (out of Coire na Ciste). This is crossed, and the hut, situated on the crest of a blunt spur between the streams, is about a hundred metres above.

Starting from the Youth Hostel, this approach is only slightly longer than the route up the glen but in bad visibility the route-finding is more difficult and after a big snowfall the saddle and traverse into the glen are very prone to heavy drifting and possible avalanche below the Castle area, 2 - 2^1/$_2$ hours.

Other approaches to the North-East face: there are two alternative variations (with little to choose between them) starting from the large car park at the end of the Glen Nevis road. Both are exceptionally steep and are unsuitable for use as a means of reaching the C.I.C. Hut and not recommended for reaching the majority of climbs. But in good visibility for the fit valley-based climber, they give the quickest approach to the Little Brenva Face or the normal route on North-East Buttress.

(a)   From the car park take a diagonal line up the hillside to reach the saddle between Meall Cumhann and Ben Nevis and then follow the ridge in a north-westerly direction. Finally, when the steep ridge merges into the easier angled slopes above, veer slightly right to gain the Carn Mor Dearg Arête at the Abseil Post Sign (GR 171710) (2-2½ hours). Descend into Coire Leis by the easiest line. If approaching routes on the Little Brenva Face, a traverse left from the col leads in five minutes to the foot of 'Bob Run'. Beware of avalanches on this traverse line.

(b)   Climb straight up above the car park follow the bank (right-east) of the waterslide of Allt Coire Eoghainn. Once over the lip of the Coire, head up to the right (north-east) to join the previous route on the ridge two hundred metres below the Carn Mor Dearg Arête (2- 2½ hours). Care should be exercised on this route as many fatal accidents have occurred on the slabs at the top of the waterslide.

(c)   From the Steall Hut the best way is to join route (a) at the Meall Cumhann saddle. Follow a small indefinite track which leaves upper Glen Nevis immediately above the entrance to the gorge, and makes a rising traverse above it, crossing the flank of Meall Cumhann until it is possible to strike up to the saddle. Alternatively one may follow the Allt Coire Guibhsachan (above the ruin of the old Steall GR 186687), by the left (west) bank and head directly up the westward branch corrie to gain the Carn Mor Dearg Arête. However, there are great areas of slab in this corrie which can be very difficult under icy conditions. Also descent from the Carn Mor Dearg Arête into Coire Leis is difficult and only recommended from the Abseil Post Sign area.

DESCENTS FROM BEN NEVIS

(See front end paper map)

The high summit plateau of Ben Nevis is surrounded on nearly all sides by steep and difficult ground. Many accidents have occurred in descent. Often this part of the day will call for more concentration and shrewdness of judgement than at any other time.

The best descent will be determined not only by your point of arrival on the summit plateau but also by the weather and snow conditions. The shortest way will not necessarily be the best and in really bad conditions the only safe way off the mountain may be by Route 1 below; long and tiresome though it may be. Careful use of map and compass and the sketch plan of the cliffs given in this guidebook will suffice to get you down but local knowledge is invaluable. When visibility is good, make a close study of the general topography of the mountain and if possible visit the summit plateau with a view to memorising its details. The ruined observatory, topped by a survival shelter, is an unmistakable landmark on the summit itself even though the neighbouring triangulation point and numerous cairns may be obliterated in a hard winter.

The best aids to descending from the summit of Ben Nevis are the O.S. Map, Outdoor Leisure 32, Mountainmaster of Ben Nevis, 1:25,000 and a compass, and the ability to use both in vile weather conditions. These two items should form essential companions to this guidebook. The insert on that map (Scale 1:10,000) is particularly useful. It shows the sharply indented plateau, and the gullies which must be avoided on compass bearings in poor visibility. Anyone who visits the mountains in summer or winter without a map and a compass (and the ability to use them in 'white out') is putting their life at risk.

Using the map previously mentioned the following descents are recommended:

1. Red Burn

The easiest and safest way down the mountain. Follow a grid bearing of 231 degrees for 150 metres from the summit (use a rope to measure it if you are not sure how many double paces you take to a hundred metres). This will avoid the steep drop of Gardyloo Gully close on your right. Then a bearing of 281 degrees (grid). Don't forget to convert your grid bearings to magnetic (approx. + 5 degrees in 1990). On this last bearing you should reach continuously steeper ground after 800 metres of downhill travel. At this point the 'Tourist' route meets the plateau. Continue on down an easy slope, for another kilometre, then turn north towards 'Halfway-Lochan'.

N.B. Along this route it is important not to stray left (south) in the first two kilometres, as this would lead to the steep and serious ground of 'Five Finger Gully'.

The Red Burn is well known as a good 'Bum Slide'. Please be aware that large waterfalls exist at the bottom of the burn before it reaches the track and many large rocks are present all the way up the burn which will not only rip your expensive Goretex pants, but may put a hole in your head as well! This area does avalanche from time to time also.

2. No.4 Gully

For climbers returning to the C.I.C. Hut or Allt a'Mhuilinn area, this descent is straightforward in good visibility. The top of the gully has a metal marker post with the number 4 drilled into it (GR 158717). Sometimes the cornice can be impassable, but a slot is usually dug out from below. Also it is possible at times to move a few metres to the north, along the rim and gain access to the gully down steeper ground. Avalanches have occurred in this gully from time to time and the initial entry can be steep, but it soon eases. Take care.

N.B. A bearing due west from the lip of this gully (270 degrees grid) is a safe descent to Glen Nevis.

3. Carn Mor Dearg Arête / Abseil Post Sign

This route can be used with care. It provides a method of descending quickly to a lower altitude, especially if the weather on the plateau is fierce. MANY DEATHS HAVE OCCURRED ON THIS DESCENT OVER THE YEARS. Most of the fatalities have been connected with people straying too far left (north) from the summit in descent.

From the summit trig point a bearing of 134 degrees (grid) should be held. Initially the ground will be flat. After 100 metres the gradient steepens abruptly and some short posts may be seen, keep these to your left (north-east). From the steepening after approximately 200 metres of descent a slight col will be found to the left (east) half a kilometre from the summit. At this point is a metal sign (GR 171710) with information relating to the 'Abseil Posts'. Only two of these posts remain (winter 1990) and with care the person experienced in negotiating Grade 1 ground in descent will be able to move down easily but steeply into Coire Leis. Often it is easier to traverse left (west) towards the Little Brenva Face, before descending. However, snow build-up will dictate the easiest and most obvious route down. The angle is steep at first, but eases after 150 metres. As with many snowy descents be careful after strong winds and during periods of heavy drifting to avoid being another avalanche victim on this slope.

N.B. From the Abseil Post Sign it is possible to descend to the head of Glen Nevis on a bearing of 220 degrees (grid). This leads to the top of the 'Waterslide' mentioned elsewhere under approaches. The original bearing of 134° (grid) from the summit should not be followed for more than 500 metres as it leads to steep and dangerous ground.

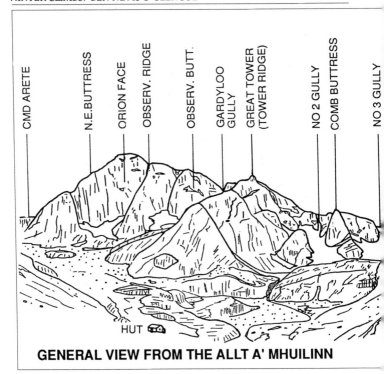

GENERAL VIEW FROM THE ALLT A' MHUILINN

Extra Tips:

For those climbers 'topping out' on the following routes in poor visibility and not wishing to visit the summit, these bearing will help:

Tower Ridge	214° grid for 130 metres then	281° grid to Red Burn
Tower Gully	214° grid for 50 metres then	281° grid to Red Burn
Gardyloo Buttress	214° grid for 75 metres then	281° grid to Red Burn
No.2 Gully	281° grid to Red Burn	
No.3 Gully	281° grid to Red Burn	
Green/Comb Gully	220° grid for 150 metres then	281° grid to Red Burn

For climbers finishing on routes to the east of the summit (N.E.

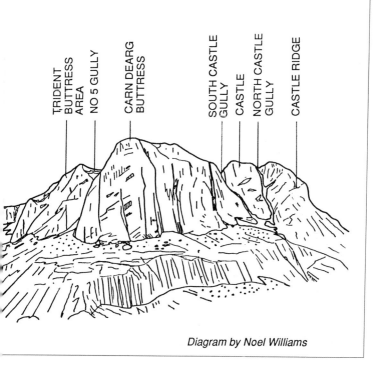

Diagram by Noel Williams

Buttress and Little Brenva Face) it is advisable to try and find the summit as a definite reference point before descending if they are unsure about the descent. To do this, it should be possible to use the N.E. edge of the plateau above Zero, Point Five and Hadrian's Wall as a 'handrail' to the summit. Cornice collapse has caused a few fatalities in this area so stay roped, with only one member of the party near the edge.

BEN NEVIS - GENERAL TOPOGRAPHY

The northerly faces of Ben Nevis and Carn Dearg N.W. form one continuous complex of cliffs which attain a maximum height of 500m

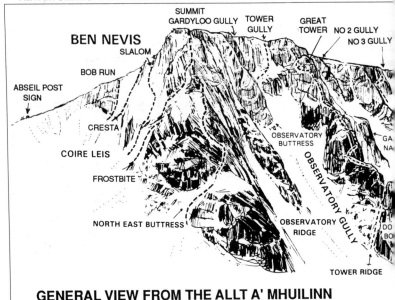

GENERAL VIEW FROM THE ALLT A' MHUILINN

and extend for 3½kms overlooking the upper part of the Allt a'Mhuilinn glen. It is the most impressive mountain face in the British Isles. The incomparable classic ridges are flanked by formidable walls leading back into deeply recessed corries which themselves contain numerous large buttresses and gullies. The scale is so vast that it is difficult to appreciate, particularly on first acquaintance.

Walking up the glen of the Allt a'Mhuilinn, the first feature the climber will see on the right is Castle Ridge and its flanking North Wall. Beyond this and at a higher level is the recess of Castle Corrie which contains the Castle itself, its two demarcating gullies and to the left of these the tapering pillar of Raeburn's Buttress. The cliffs then jut out again. The left-hand side of the Castle Corrie is known as the North Wall of Carn Dearg; this cliff connects with a 300m prow of compact rock, a truncated spur, the Great Buttress of Carn Dearg. Waterfall Gully is the dividing line between these last two. Round the corner of the Great Buttress is No.5 Gully, set at a reasonable angle

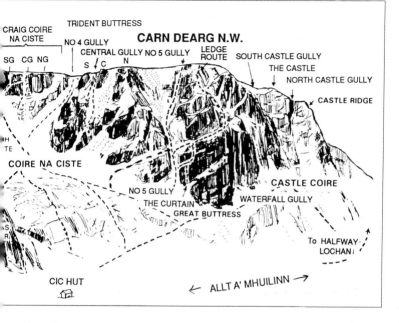

CRAIG COIRE NA CISTE — TRIDENT BUTTRESS — **CARN DEARG N.W.** — NO 4 GULLY — CENTRAL GULLY — NO 5 GULLY — LEDGE ROUTE — SOUTH CASTLE GULLY — THE CASTLE — NORTH CASTLE GULLY — CASTLE RIDGE — SG CG NG — S ↓ C N — COIRE NA CISTE — NO 5 GULLY — THE CURTAIN — GREAT BUTTRESS — CASTLE COIRE — WATERFALL GULLY — To HALFWAY LOCHAN — CIC HUT — ← ALLT A' MHUILINN →

but almost 500m in length. Ledge Route comes out of No.5 Gully to gain the crest of the ridge at the top of the Great Buttress and follows this to the summit of Carn Dearg. To the left (east) of the Great Buttress the cliffs fall back to form the great amphitheatre of Coire na Ciste, the floor of which at over 900m is a wild and magnificent place to visit. There are three relatively easy exits from the head of the corrie; No.4 Gully (hidden) on the right; No.3 Gully apparently the lowest col in the centre and No.2 Gully which disappears to the left of the prominent buttress of the Comb. Tower Ridge is the next main feature and is one of the most important on the mountain. Narrow and very long, it projects for 1½kms from the summit plateau into the glen to terminate abruptly as the Douglas Boulder immediately above the hut. From the foot of the boulder (215m in itself!) there is a vertical rise of over 550m before the junction with the plateau.

To the east of Tower Ridge is the long slope of Observatory Gully which branches in its upper quarter to form Gardyloo and Tower

Gullies. Observatory Gully, broad in its lower part and tapering as it rises for 500m is only an approach to other climbs and can be regarded almost as a deep corrie. Rising to the left of the gully are some of the most formidable climbs on the mountain: The Minus Gullies and Buttresses and the Orion Face (all on the flank of North East Buttress); Zero Gully which lies in the corner between Orion Face and the long spur of Observatory Ridge and finally Point Five Gully and Observatory Buttress.

The final great ridge almost at the head of the glen is called the North East Buttress. It is again a massive projection, almost 500m in vertical height, but is steeper and therefore not as long as Tower Ridge. Below the First Platform it terminates in a great rock nose not unlike the Douglas Boulder. The Allt a'Mhuilinn glen ends in Coire Leis below the col of the Carn Mor Dearg Arête. Overlooking this corrie is the east flank of the North East Buttress; now generally referred to as the Little Brenva Face.

The climbs are described from east to west (left to right) corrie by corrie.

CLIMBS FROM COIRE LEIS

Coire Leis is the basin at the head of the Allt a'Mhuilinn glen. From the C.I.C. Hut follow the right bank of the burn until opposite the lowest rocks below the First Platform North East Buttress, then traverse up the right-hand side of the corrie beneath the east face (about 1 hour from the C.I.C. Hut).

Although all the routes on the Little Brenva follow fairly arbitrary lines they are very popular. The face is alpine in character, receives the full benefit of any sun and consequently often becomes heavily iced. Generally the climbs are long and give some interesting route finding; considerable difficulty may be experienced in misty conditions.

Bob-run   130m   Grade II
I.Clough, D.Pipes and party   10th February 1959
Commences almost at the level of the col of the Carn Mor Dearg Arête and follows a couloir in the left extremity of the face. Start to the right of a buttress and climb 30m of ice or iced rocks to gain the couloir. After another 30m the route curls round to the left by either of two

Comb Gully (III/IV), Climber: Trevor Jones Photo: Alan Kimber
Looking down the crux pitch of Point Five Gully (V)
Climber: Nick Halls Photo: Alan Kimber

variations, both of which generally give at least one further pitch on ice.

Moonwalk   270m   Grade III/IV
K.Hughes and J.Mothersele   March 1973
Start 10m left of Cresta below an ice pitch which can vary in difficulty depending on conditions. Climb the ice above and continue over a snow slope to the foot of an ice pitch formed by a rock corner (100m). Climb the ice above to another snow slope (45m). Move up to a steep ice wall (45m). Climb this for 15m and an ice groove to snow-ice field (35m). Cross rightwards to belay below rock wall (45m). Traverse horizontally right below the wall to a steep rock arête which is followed to the summit slopes.
N.B. Many variations are possible in this area and escapes left (south) can be made with care towards Bob-Run.

Cresta Climb   275m   Graded II/III**
T.W.Patey, L.S.Lovat and A.G.Nichol   16th February 1957
The main feature of this route is a 180m shallow couloir which commences above and to the left of a 90m rocky spur and finishes amongst the small cliffs at the exit from the highest part of the left-hand side of the face. The original start was from the right but it is now more usual to commence to the left of the rocky spur and about 30m right of Bob-Run. 30m of icy rocks (or ice) are climbed to gain a long broad snow shelf. A small gully leads up from the right-hand side of the shelf to reach the couloir proper which is followed to its termination in an ice basin. Traverse up to the right to gain an easy snow slope which leads out to a finish about 50m from the top of N.E. Buttress.

Slalom   275m   Grade II/III**
D.Pipes, I.Clough, J.M.Alexander, R.Shaw and A.Flegg   6th January 1959
The upper part of the right-hand side of the face is a steep rock wall, the Central Spur. Both Slalom and Frostbite start in the bay below this wall and to the right of a 100m. rocky spur.
   Slalom starts up a shallow tongue of snow from the left of the bay and zig-zags up through rock bluffs towards the middle of the wall

In the exit chimneys of Orion Face Direct (V) Climber: Nick Halls

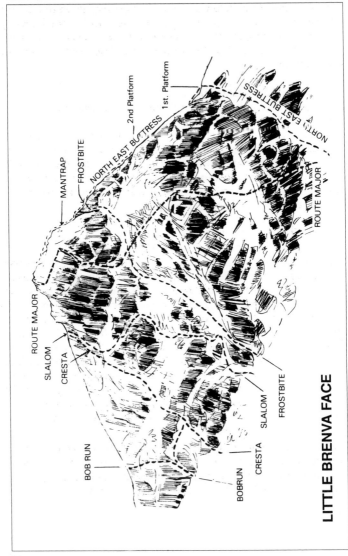

LITTLE BRENVA FACE

of the Central Spur. Below the Spur a long rising leftwards traverse is made to gain an easy snow slope which leads to the foot of a rocky ridge overlooking the couloir of Cresta. The rocks usually give the crux of the climb and lead to the final easy exit slope which is shared with Cresta.

Frostbite   275m   Grade III
I.Clough, D.Pipes, J.M.Alexander, P.A.Hannon and M.Bucke
February 1958
Starts from the above mentioned bay and follows an Icy groove up to the right to gain a 120m snow field. Follow this rightwards and cross a rocky ridge below the nose of the Central Spur proper to gain further snow slopes slanting rightwards under the Spur. These eventually lead out onto the crest of the N.E. Buttress below the Mantrap, (see N.E. Buttress Route).

Route Major   300m   Grade III**
H.MacInnes and I.Clough   16th February 1969
Not an easy route to find and follow, but for those people who enjoy exploring middle grade mixed ground, an excellent route when in condition. The route generally follows the line of a summer climb (Eastern Climb). To get a good look at the route it is advisable to walk up the east side of Coire Leis above the hut until opposite the start of N.E.Buttress. A hanging ice-field high on the face is a key feature towards which climbers should aim. A start from the traverse line (left end) onto the First Platform of N.E. Buttress can be made. Follow ice ribs up the wall to gain a snow slope crossed by Frostbite. Cross this and continue up the buttress by a chimney line going right (difficult route finding). Where the route goes close to the Mantrap of N.E. Buttress break out left on a horizontal traverse then up various small snowfields to the top.

N.B. An alternative start to the climb can be made by walking up directly under N.E. Buttress and continuing until the ground levels out as it approaches upper Coire Leis. From here turn up right and commence climbing. This start is well right of Frostbite.

Newbigging's Route - Far Right Variation   180m   Grade IV
R.Campbell, R.Carrington and J.R.Marshall   February 1972
This route is on the triangular face which falls vertically into Coire
Leis as one walks beneath the First Platform of N.E. Buttress. It starts
10m left of the rocky edge of the face (this edge forms the north and
east facets of the buttress) and runs parallel to that edge. The route is
a natural winter line and easily seen on approaching the hut. Follow
the big corner groove and slabs, passing an overhang on the left. The
main difficulties are in the lower 60m. In lean conditions with poor
icing this route can be serious.

North East Buttress   500m   Grade III/IV***
W.W.Naismith, W.Brunskill, A.B.W.Kennedy, W.W.King and F.C.Squance
April 1896
The normal winter route avoids the rocks below the First Platform by
going up into Coire Leis until a broad easy shelf leads back up to the
right to the First Platform. Shortly above the Platform the rocks on the
crest become very steep and the easiest route is to traverse an exposed
ledge on the right until a gully leads back up to the left to reach the
small Second Platform. Alternatively the steep step may be turned on
the left or even taken direct. Above the Second Platform the ridge is
followed, turning obstacles, until a smooth blunt 5m nose bars the
way. This is the notorious Mantrap which can be extremely difficult
in icy conditions. It is best turned on the right by a slight descent and
traverse to a scoop. This leads to the foot of a steep corner which again
can be very hard. It may be best to move slightly down to the left until,
not far above the top of the Mantrap, a shallow chimney leads up to
the left of the ridge crest on to easier ground. This upper part of the
route is normally the crux of the climb, but the major difficulties are
relatively short and it is not too far to the top; probably better to force
the route than be faced with the long retreat.

CLIMBS FROM OBSERVATORY GULLY

Very large avalanches fall from the upper reaches of this gully. It
would be wise to avoid the climbs at the top end of this gully after
heavy snowfall, strong winds or during a thaw.

Slingsby's Chimney   125m   Grade II
A direct approach to the First Platform of N.E.Buttress from the west.
To the right of the slabby rocks of the nose leading to the First
Platform is an obvious shallow gully fault. This gives the climb.

Beneath the First Platform of N.E. Buttress and to the left of
Slingsby's Chimney is a considerable area of steep ground, easily
seen on the hut approach up the Allt a'Mhuilinn. The following two
routes are located in this area.

Green Hollow Route   200m   Grade IV
J.R.Marshall and J.Moriarty   February 1965
Start at the lowest rocks on the left (often snow-covered) and trend
diagonally up righwards by iced slabs and grooves towards a large
snow bay, high up in the middle of the face, The Green Hollow. From
the highest point of the bay climb an iced slab left onto the final arête.
Follow this easily to the top of the First Platform.

Raeburn's 18 Minute Route   140m   Grade II
Start 6m left of Slingsby's Chimney and follow the line of least
resistance to the First Platform.

THE MINUS AND ORION FACES

To the right of Slingsby's Chimney is a steep area of cliff. It is split by
three gullies (the Minus Gullies: Minus 3 on the left) and bounded on
the right by Zero Gully.

MINUS THREE BUTTRESS

Lies between Slingsby's Chimney and Minus Three Gully. All routes
escapable.

Right-hand Wall Route   140m   Grade IV
R.Ferguson and J.Higham   March 1972
Just to the right of Slingsby's Chimney is a line of chimneys: follow
this line as close as possible, the final slabby part below the First

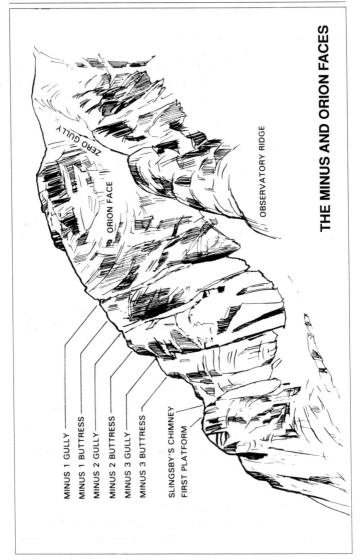

THE MINUS AND ORION FACES

ZERO GULLY

ORION FACE

OBSERVATORY RIDGE

MINUS 1 GULLY
MINUS 1 BUTTRESS
MINUS 2 GULLY
MINUS 2 BUTTRESS
MINUS 3 GULLY
MINUS 3 BUTTRESS
SLINGSBY'S CHIMNEY
FIRST PLATFORM

Platform giving the crux.

Wagroochimsla   140m   Grade IV
S.Docherty and G.Adam   January 1972
Start between Right-hand Wall and Platform's Rib and climb left to
the central bulge; climbed with aid on first ascent. Continue rightwards to the Second Platform.

Platform's Rib   150m   Grade IV
H.MacInnes, I.Clough, T.Sullivan and M.White   8th March 1959
Follow the rib to the left of Minus Three Gully until part of the gully
is used before moving back left to the North East Buttress.

Minus Three Gully   160m   Grade IV***
R.Smith and J.Marshall   7th February 1960
When in condition, a classic. Climb steep snow to a cave belay, climb
steep ice on the left and continue by a groove to snow. Another steep
pitch leads to easier climbing and North East Buttress.

MINUS TWO BUTTRESS

To the right of Minus Three Gully is a slabby buttress, interrupted at
about one third height by overhangs and forming a prominent ridge
on the left. Bounded to the right by Minus Two Gully.

Left-hand Route   270m   Grade VI*
S.Docherty and N.Muir   30th January 1972
Start immediately right of Minus Three Gully and ascend the ridge
for 65m to an overlap. Descend 6m then swing round a rib and up a
snow arête to a belay below an overhang. From a peg in the overhang
tension to the slab's edge and up to belay on right wall. Steep ice leads
to an easier section of slabby rocks and eventually to Second Platform.

Central Route   270m   Grade VI
A.Nisbet and B.Sprunt   18th March 1979
The climb follows a line just to the right of the previous route to the
overhangs. These are gained by a righward traverse and turned on

THE MINUS AND ORION FACES

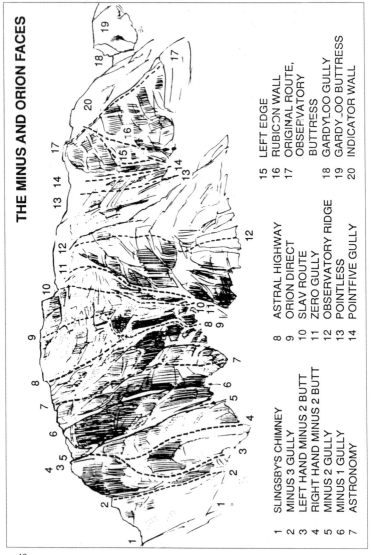

1   SLINGSBY'S CHIMNEY
2   MINUS 3 GULLY
3   LEFT HAND MINUS 2 BUTT
4   RIGHT HAND MINUS 2 BUTT
5   MINUS 2 GULLY
6   MINUS 1 GULLY
7   ASTRONOMY

8   ASTRAL HIGHWAY
9   ORION DIRECT
10 SLAV ROUTE
11 ZERO GULLY
12 OBSERVATORY RIDGE
13 POINTLESS
14 POINTFIVE GULLY

15 LEFT EDGE
16 RUBICON WALL
17 ORIGINAL ROUTE,
    OBSERVATORY
    BUTTRESS
18 GARDYLOO GULLY
19 GARDY_OO BUTTRESS
20 INDICATOR WALL

the right using aid to reach easier ground.
N.B. First ascent took a very long time!

Right-hand Route   270m   Grade VI*
R.Carrington and A.Rouse   March 1972
To the right of the prominent ridge is a large slabby corner. Climb the
corner and gain the easier angled upper section of the buttress with
difficulty. Slabs and grooves lead to the North East Buttress.

Minus Two Buttress   270m   Grade V*
B.Dunn, C.Higgins and D.McArthur   5th March 1974
Start 13m to the left of Minus Two Gully and go up an icefall then
right to an open book corner. Climb all of the corner to a prominent
snow crest. Traverse a snow ramp leftwards and climb an iced gully
line to the North East Buttress.

Minus Two Gully   270m   Grade V***
J.Marshall, J.Stenhouse and D.Haston   11th February 1959
A fine climb when in condition. A long pitch of snow and ice leads to
a belay below an overhang. Avoid the overhang by a detour to the left
and regain the upper chimneys leading to the North East Buttress.

MINUS ONE BUTTRESS

The narrow buttress to the right of Minus Two Gully and bounded on
its right by Minus One Gully.

Minus One Buttress   290m   Grade VI***
N.Muir and A.Paul   5th April 1977
Start at the centre of the buttress, at a corner, and follow the easiest
line to the overhangs at 100m. Move across rightwards and follow the
buttress, fairly close to Minus One Gully to the North East Buttress.
Fine open buttress climbing.

Minus One Gully   290m   Grade V/VI***
K.Crocket and C.Stead   1974
The hardest of the Nevis gullies. Easy climbing leads to an ice wall
giving access to a cave below the main overhang. Avoid the overhang

on the left before regaining the gully above. Continue past a snow bay to the North East Buttress.

THE ORION FACE

This area of the mountain lies immediately left of Zero Gully. On its left and lower down is the toe of the buttress which takes the line of Astronomy. This buttress projects into the approach slopes leading to Orion Face. The bottom of the face is a steep icefall with the Great Slab Rib to the left. Above and right of this rib is an obvious feature known as The Basin. At the top left side of The Basin is a steep icy exit known as Epsilon Chimney. Up right of this Basin is the Second Slab Rib which is often the only feature showing in the middle of the face when snow and ice obliterate all other detail. Higher up is another smaller basin snow patch and left of this at a higher level, the exit chimney.

Astronomy   300m   Grade V
H.MacInnes, A.Fyffe and K.Spence   March 1970
Start about 16m to the right of Minus One Gully and climb twin cracks to leftward slanting snow patches. These snow patches lead to a groove. Climb the groove and go right to a large corner. Up the corner then move right, then back left by walls and grooves. Skirt left below the upper rocks and escape by descending into the top of Minus One gully (or follow the next route which gives a better finish).

Astronomy, Direct Finish   120m   Grade V**
T.Saunders and M.Fowler   March 1986
Instead of skirting left below the upper rocks into Minus One Gully, trend slightly right to belay below the right-hand end of the steep upper rocks. Gain the crest of the buttress on the right and climb an iced slab, trending right to gain a fine ice groove near the crest of the buttress. Follow this steeply to easier ground.
(Author's note: Tim Jepson and Roger Baxter-Jones climbed a similar line in the late seventies.)

Smith-Holt Route   420m   Grade V**
R.Smith and R.Holt   *January 1959*
Starts left of Orion Direct and climbs leftward facing corners immediately left of the Great Slab Rib, until it is possible to cut back right into The Basin with difficulty. From The Basin the steep and icy Epsilon Chimney is taken and exit made easily via a ledge leading up left to the crest of N.E.Buttress at a 'V' notch. A great route which avoids the queues on Orion Direct.

Urban Spaceman   350m   Grade V***
D.Hawthorn and A.Paul   *April 1983*
This route lies on the buttress between Astronomy and Orion Direct in its lower section, and left of Epsilon Chimney in the upper part. Start as for Orion Direct and move left to gain the Great Slab Rib which is climbed direct for two pitches (30m & 40m). Move up right to gain grooves at 30m. Follow these for two pitches to the steep upper section (30m & 20m). Move right over slabs to a good stance (30m). Climb steep ice-filled chimney and mixed ground (45m). Two further pitches lead to the crest of N.E. Buttress. An excellent route when conditions are good.

Orion Direct   420m   Grade V***
R.Smith and J.Marshall   *13th February 1960*
A classic: the technical difficulty is often low but in such conditions belays are usually poor. Climb to the left end of a broad ledge stretching out from Zero Gully and take a steep chimney line above until an upward traverse left leads to The Basin. It is possible to continue direct to The Basin from the chimney but harder. Move up rightwards to an obvious rock rib (Second Slab Rib) and take this by the face to the right, or by a longer traverse right below the face. Trend up leftwards in three pitches to finish in the steep icy exit chimneys.

Astral Highway   240m   Grade V***
C.Higgins and A.Kimber   *28th December 1976*
A direct finish from The Basin starting at the top of The Basin, left of centre at the groove right of Epsilon Chimney. Gain the groove and climb it and successive grooves to reach the North East Buttress.

On Orion Face Direct (V) Climbers seen in the background are on Zero Gully (V). Climber: Alan Kimber

Zybernaught   240m   Grade V
D.Hawthorn and A.Paul
Follows a set of zig-zag grooves between Epsilon Chimney and Astral Highway. From the foot of Epsilon Chimney move up right and below steep bulge (45m). Climb bulge and ground above to left trending groove (45m). Follow groove to open corner (45m). Climb corner and ground above to North East Buttress.

Journey into Space   240m   Grade V**
A.Kimber and C.Higgins   8th March 1980
Start midway between Astral Highway and Second Slab Rib. Climb directly to the right of a short corner where a delicate traverse right gives easier climbing. Climb diagonally leftwards by an obvious iced slab until a break right can be made onto the upper section of the wall. Climb slab, move right beneath overhang then by groove direct, climbing occasional bulge until right end of prominent snowfield is reached. Move diagonally left up snowfield (possible to finish direct) and climb obvious corner to finish.

Slav Route   420m   Grade V*
D.Lang and N.Quinn   23rd March 1974

Takes a line just to the left of Zero Gully, but completely independent. An obvious icefall at 50m is usually avoided to the left but may be climbed with difficulty. Near the top an exit can be made into Zero Gully but a line slightly leftwards is taken.

Zero Gully   300m   Grade V***
H.MacInnes, A.Nichol and I .Puley   18th February 1957

The easiest but most serious of the big three classics: the lack of belays meriting the V grade. Climb the gully to a stance below a left facing chimney to the left of the main gully. Ascend the chimney then traverse right to an amphitheatre in the gully. Take the narrow gully above to easy ground by a long pitch.

N.B. An alternative start can be made to Zero Gully by climbing the steep ice on the right, thus avoiding the rightward traverse higher up. This option varies with conditions. Also, as with many other steep gully lines Zero is not a nice place to be when breezes on the summit deposit vast quantities of powder snow down the climb! Beware of debris from other parties.

OBSERVATORY RIDGE

The ridge itself is the narrow buttress to the right of Zero Gully but as an area is taken to stretch to Point Five Gully.

East Face   166m   Grade IV
B.Dunn and C.Higgins   3rd March 1974

Below and to the right of Zero Gully, the left side of Observatory Ridge is split by a line of grooves which give the route, until they merge into the ridge itself.

Silverside   115m   Grade IV*
B.Dunn and D.Gardner   17th April 1977

Start 16m below East Face and move up rightwards over snow and iced grooves to the left end of a large ledge. Traverse left and climb left slanting line to a snow bay and easier ground.

N.B. The above two climbs finish up the following route.

Observatory Ridge   420m   Grade III/IV***
H.Raeburn, F.Goggs and W.Mounsey   April 1920
The finest and most difficult of the classic ridges, the line of the route generally follows the crest of the ridge. The lowest buttress normally gives the most serious problems. The easiest line is to gain a shelf on the left flank one third of the way up this buttress and then work obliquely rightwards to the crest. Above this difficulties can be turned and the upper part of Zero Gully is often taken for the final 150m.

Abacus   106m   Grade IV*
N.Muir and A.Paul   27th November 1977
The route climbs the obvious bow-shaped chimney groove in the middle of the face between Observatory Ridge and Hadrian's Wall to reach the ridge.

Observatory Wall   90m   Grade IV
D.Hawthorn and A.Paul   November 1985
A crackline left of Abacus has been climbed. It has a cave at half-height. Climb to the cave by slabs and exit left and up cracks to the crest of the ridge.

Antonine Wall   150m   Grade IV*
N.Muir and A.Paul   3rd December 1977
Just right of Abacus is a steep ice-filled groove leading to a slab capped by a huge roof. Climb the groove to below the roof and move right over slabs to a snow groove leading to the crest.
N.B. The last three routes are good bad weather routes, as it is possible to descend by abseil as did the first ascentionists.

Vade Mecum   320m   Grade IV/V
(Previously referred to as West Face Direct)
D.Knowles, D.Wilson and party   1974
Start just left of the ice-smear of Hadrian's Wall, and climb over slabby mixed ground to an obvious pointed block. Move left and finish by a steep ice-pillar to Observatory Ridge.

Hadrian's Wall Direct   320m   Grade IV***
M.Geddes and G.Little   April 1971

Between Observatory Ridge and Point Five Gully is a very obvious ice-smear. Nowhere steep, this popular climb is rather poorly protected lower down (poor belay stance after first pitch). Climb the smear in two or three pitches to a chimney with good belay. Take the chimney to a snow patch and gain Observatory Ridge after two long pitches.

Sickle   300m   Grade V*
B.Hall and M.Geddes   December 1977

Start to the right of Hadrian's Wall and move up leftwards to climb a groove parallel with, and close to, Hadrian's Wall; then go back right to continue by a steep ice corner to join Hadrian's Wall at the snow patch, just above the chimney.

Galactic Hitchhiker   300m   VI**
M.Geddes and C.Higgins   14th April 1978

One of the first Grade VI's climbed on Ben Nevis. Right of Hadrian's Wall the main feature is the rightward stepped corner system above the great slab left of Point Five. Climb just left of the centre of the slab to a small nose (50m). Move up right into the main groove system beneath the corner. Traverse right above the slab in an exposed position via a pointed block to belay on the right. Continue above by very steep and difficult walls and ledges right of the main corner system to easier ground which is followed to the top.

N.B. An easier start can be made on the left and nearer to Sickle, followed by a traverse right to a pointed block.

Pointless   300m   Grade V**
N.Banks and G.Smith   19th February 1978

A difficult climb, especially on the second pitch, where a grade of VI may be more appropriate. Start on the obvious slab close to the left side of Point Five Gully. Follow the right edge of the slab towards a rock barrier which is level with the normal first belay of Point Five Gully (bottom of the chimney). Trend up left at the rock barrier to a spike belay beneath a steep obvious corner (50m). Climb the corner with difficulty (possible peg on left wall) and trend right at the top.

HADRIAN'S WALL TO POINT FIVE GULLY

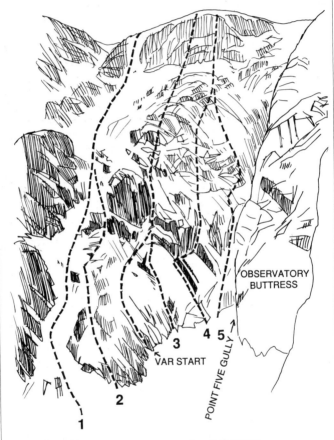

OBSERVATORY
BUTTRESS

4 5

3

VAR START

2

POINT FIVE GULLY

1

1	HADRIAN'S WALL	4	POINTLESS
2.	SICKLE	5.	INTERSTELLAR
3.	GALACTIC HITCHHIKER		OVERDRIVE

Continue directly for two interesting (III) pitches. Easier climbing leads in three pitches to the plateau rim.

N.B. As with many ice climbs the first pitch of this route may be longer if the build-up at the base of the cliff is lacking.

Interstellar Overdrive   300m   Grade V
I.Kennedy and R.Anderson   March 1980
Climb the left-hand rib of Point Five to belay below a wall (30m). Go right across the wall until immediately above Point Five. Follow a groove running left to a chimney, which is the right side of an enormous perched block. Climb the chimney to a belay on top of the block (40m). Climb a corner and ice wall rightwards above to a ledge in a snow bay (40m), followed by a groove on the right, which trends back left to meet Pointless above the difficult section (40m).

Point Five Gully   325m   Grade V***
I.Clough, D.Pipes, R.Shaw and J.Alexander   12th-16th January 1959
A justifiably popular route. The standard Grade V from which all other steep snow/ice gully climbs are gauged. The main difficulties are encountered on the first three pitches. A left trending slab of ice leads to good belays on the left beneath a step chimney (45m). The steep chimney to an overhung recess, belay on the right (45m). A final steepening slab leading to a bulging narrow finish (45m). Follow the gully above easily with one steeper section (II/III) to pass the cornice on the right. Beware of falling debris from other parties and spindrift avalanches.

N.B. For climbers on top form and requiring more excitement, it is recommended that they take to the left wall of the gully after the third hard pitch. Find your own way to the top at about Grade III/IV depending on the line chosen.

OBSERVATORY BUTTRESS

This is the final, upper part of the great left wall of Observatory Gully. It stretches rightwards from Point Five Gully to Gardyloo Gully (which forms the obvious exit gully at the top left of Observatory Gully). From the foot of Gardyloo Gully an initially broad terrace cuts leftwards across the upper part of Observatory Buttress, narrowing as it goes. The face above the right side of this terrace is called Indicator Wall: the face being bounded on the left by the short gully of Good Friday Climb.

Pointblank   325m   Grade VI
M.Duff and J.Tinker   4th March 1984
(Direct version 2nd ascent, as described)
M.Duff and R.Nowack   24th February 1988
Climbs the buttress immediately right of Point Five Gully. Start four metres below the foot of Point Five and climb a small steep groove left of Left Edge Route to the snow patch of that route. From the left edge of the snow patch move up right to corner and belay (25m). Climb the right-hand groove/crack above and thin icy slabs to a corner and capping roof. Semi-hanging stance on pegs (22m). Three metres below the stance on the right enter a short groove which is climbed to a narrow chimney crack. Follow this crack to a roof and go diagonally left till overlooking Point Five Gully. Climb directly via a steep groovy ramp and wall to a snow bay and ledge system. Belay on rounded spike (43m).

N.B. It is possible to avoid the hanging stance on the second pitch and thus arrive at the snow bay, by using a 70m rope as did the 2nd ascent party. Right of the belay climb a sloping groove and more easily above to a series of steps (40m). Follow a series of indistinct corners and steps to the crest on the right of Point Five Gully. The upper section of this climb and small parts of the lower pitches had previously been climbed by Dave Wilkinson on a variant ascent of Left Edge Route.

Left Edge Route   360m   Grade V*
D.Lang and N.Quinn   9th March 1974
Start at the foot of Point Five gully and climb a rib to a snow patch. Climb the left-hand groove above then move up right to an ice-fall which is followed to the terrace. Move right along the terrace and finish by Ordinary Route (see below).

Matchpoint   325m   Grade V
S.Richardson and E.Hart   29th March 1986
Between Left Edge and Rubicon Wall are two left facing corner

systems. Climb the right-hand one (50m). Climb a short steep snow slope to an overhanging, inverted triangular wall. Traverse left and climb an icicle fringe to a snowfield. Climb the right-hand icefall above to the terrace (the left-hand one being on Left Edge Route), and continue up the buttress as for Left Edge Route.

Rubicon Wall 340m Grade V**
N Muir and A.Paul 14th April 1977
Start about 20m right of Left Edge Route and take a more or less direct line up to the terrace. Finish as for Left Edge Route.

Direct Route 340m Grade IV**
D.Stewart and W.Foster 23rd March 1952
Ascend rightwards on snow patches and short walls, starting not far to the right of Rubicon Wall, to join Ordinary Route above its main difficulties.

Ordinary Route 340m Grade IV***
J.Marshall and R.Smith February 1960
Start well to the right of Direct Route below a chimney some way up the buttress. Climb the buttress by a shallow depression to reach the chimney which usually gives the crux. From the terrace above the chimney go up leftwards to gain the final easy crest.

North-West Face 100m Grade IV
K.Crocket and C.Stead 21st March 1975
Start half-way up the right-hand side of the buttress at a bay and follow a chimney line leading to Indicator Wall, for which this route provides a good start.

INDICATOR WALL

As described in the introduction to Observatory Buttress, Indicator Wall lies above the terrace cutting the upper part of Observatory Buttress, bounded on the left by the upper gullies of Good Friday Climb and on the right by Gardyloo Gully.

Ice climbs here are the highest in the British Isles starting at 1,220m. They are fine routes when in condition and well worth the

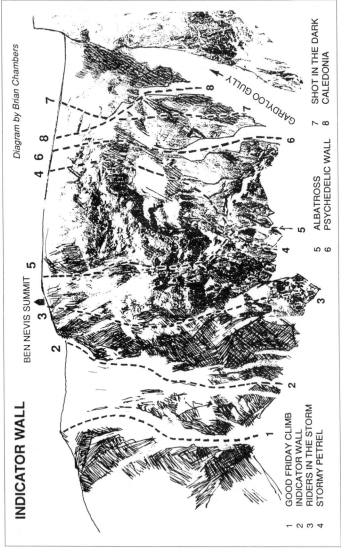

INDICATOR WALL

Diagram by Brian Chambers

BEN NEVIS SUMMIT

GARDYLOO GULLY

1 GOOD FRIDAY CLIMB
2 INDICATOR WALL
3 RIDERS IN THE STORM
4 STORMY PETREL

5 ALBATROSS
6 PSYCHEDELIC WALL

7 SHOT IN THE DARK
8 CALEDONIA

long walk. Be prepared for poorly protected leads on steep ground!

Good Friday Climb   150m   Grade III**
G.MacPhee, R.Lovel, H.Shepherd and D.Edwards   7th April 1939
Start below Gardyloo Gully and traverse left along the snow shelf until a gully can be followed for 60m where it is blocked by a wall. Go right then back left up another gully to the plateau.

Indicator Wall   180m   Grade IV**
G.Smith and T.King   February 1975
About 50m right of the gully of Good Friday is an obvious icefall on the left side of the buttress. Start at an iced-chimney groove and climb bulging ice to snow slopes topped by a gully. Climb the gully to finish at the indicator post.

Riders in the Storm   165m   Grade V
D.Hawthorn and E.Todd   April 1986
The large slab between Indicator Wall and Albatross is climbed from the lowest left-hand point of the buttress by iced grooves in two pitches of 45m and one of 30m to the top.

Albatross   150m   Grade V***
C.Higgins and M.Geddes   1978
A very open corner descends the face of the buttress about mid-way between Indicator Wall and Psychedelic Wall. Start slightly right of the main line and climb a groove for a pitch; then move back left to the main corner line. Follow this.

Stormy Petrel   160m   Grade V
D.Cuthbertson and R.Kane   1982
Climbs the big open corner right of Albatross. Climb rightwards up a shallow ramp, then direct to a rock spike beneath an overlap (30m). Go right horizontally over ribs to belay at the roof of an impressive corner (21m). Climb the left wall of the corner to large slab above. Ascend steeply right in two pitches over slabs, corners and grooves, turning a roof on the right. Belay at the foot of another corner (39m & 15m). Climb the corner then go left through bulges and right to a steep chimney and on to the final slopes, just left of Psychedelic Wall.

Psychedelic Wall   180m   Grade V***
N.Muir and A.Paul   January 1978
A direct line starting from the rocks, opposite the lowest rocks of the left edge of Gardyloo Buttress. Climb iced rocks to a snow bay (30m). Continue up steeply to gain a left trending snow ramp and from near its top take a groove leading to the left edge of a large plinth (45m). Continue up slabs, corners and chimney to the foot of a steep wall (36m & 30m). Climb the right-most of three corners to a cornice finish (39m).
N.B. On the second pitch it is possible to climb direct until 5m below an icicle fringe (belay). Climb to the icicle fringe step left and follow ice to the top.

Shot in the Dark   120m   Grade IV*
M.Geddes and A.Rouse   February 1978
On the left wall of Gardyloo Gully 30m up from the toe of the buttress and right of Psychedelic Wall route. Aim initially for the oblong roof high on the wall above. Cross several rightward slanting overlapping grooves to a short corner. Climb this then traverse right across another groove and steep slab to finish some distance right of the oblong roof.

Caledonia   150m   Grade V**
D.Gardner and A.Paul   February 1978
Climbs the steep slab corner about 60m up right of Psychedelic Wall, to gain a snow bay. Move up rightward trending snow ramp and steep slabs above, turning bulges on the right. This route finishes a little left of Shot in the Dark, left of the oblong roof.

Gardyloo Gully   170m   Grade II/III**
G.Hastings and W.P.Haskett-Smith   26th April 1897
One of the most popular routes on the mountain. The obvious direct continuation to Observatory Gully. Normally a snow slope leads to a great chockstone about 40m below the cornice. Sometimes there is a tunnel beneath the chockstone which leads to a short, steep ice pitch but in exceptional winters the whole route banks out. The cornice can be difficult.

GARDYLOO BUTTRESS

This buttress tops Observatory Gully between Gardyloo Gully on the left and Tower Gully on the right.

The cornices can be very considerable above this buttress and may be impossible to breach at times.

Left Edge   155m   Grade VI*
R.Carrington and A.Rouse   March 1976
This route requires a very good plating of ice and snow. A peg for tension was used high up to gain the upper slabs.

Start at the left edge of the buttress and climb the arête up rightwards until level with the upper chute of Smith's Route to the right (100m). Move across to the chute and finish up this.

Kellet's Route   120m   Grade VI**
A.Paul and K.Leinster   1980
The most obvious line up the buttress is the leftwards slanting icefall of Smith's Route leading to a snow chute in the upper part. Kellet's Route starts midway between Left Edge and this icefall and climbs directly to join Smith's Route (left-hand way) just below the chute.

Augean Alley   120m   Grade V**
K.Leinster, A.Paul and G.Reilly   March 1981
This route climbs Kellet's Route (see above) and finishes on the left-hand ridge bounding the finish of Smith's Route.

Smith's Route   130m   Grade V***
R.Smith and J.Marshall   8th February 1960
Climb leftwards up the obvious slanting ice grooves to a belay. Move diagonally leftwards to easier ground then back up and right to the right-hand groove. Up this to the snow chute and an easy finish. A more popular variation is to climb an icicle direct to gain the right-hand groove, which is followed to the snow chute.

If the cornice is very large it may be possible to avoid it to the left by a steep wall and narrow ridge finish.

The Great Glen   130m   Grade VI
P.Braithwaite and P.Moores   12th February 1978
The route follows the steep, shallow groove right of Smith's Route to

exit left across a gangway to belay right of Smith's Route (51m). Re-enter the groove and follow steep arête on the right to snow. (Serious - take a long rope).

Right Edge   130m   Grade III*
R.Millward and F. von Gemert   January 1977
Move up from the start of The Great Glen rightwards to gain the right arête of the buttress. Follow this to the top.

Tower Gully   120m   Grade I
G.Hastings, E.L.W. and W.P.Haskett-Smith   25th April 1897
Follow a broad snow terrace rightwards from the foot of Gardyloo Gully, below the buttress and above Tower Scoop to gain the gully proper. This is easy but the cornice is often large.

TOWER RIDGE EAST SIDE

The following 4 climbs lie on the East Side of Tower Ridge starting from the upper slopes of Observatory Gully

Tower Scoop   65m   Grade III**
I.Clough and G.Grandison   11th January 1961
Below the snow terrace which runs from the foot of Gardyloo Gully, beneath Gardyloo Buttress to Tower Gully, is a band of icy cliffs which almost block off Observatory Gully at 1,150 metres. The route follows a central ice smear in two or three pitches. Various exits are possible at the top.
N.B. To the left of this ice smear various short lines are possible, and a little harder than Tower Scoop.

Tower Cleft   75m   Grade III**
G.Pratt and J.Francis   February 1949
To the right of Tower Scoop is a deep cave-like rift formed in the angle with the east flank of Tower Ridge. This rift is the line of the route and can be very entertaining or impossible! (Move out left to escape from the rift).

Clefthanger   90m   Grade V**
D.Hawthorn and A.Paul   January 1985
Start at the foot of Tower Cleft and climb a corner system on the right wall. Climb 20m to a large ledge below a corner. Traverse right round an arête into a clean corner which is climbed passing a large dubious flake half-way on the left. Move up left by slabs, chimney and grooves.

East Wall Route   110m   Grade II/III
J.R.Marshall and R.Marshall   February 1966
Starts just downhill and to the right of Tower Cleft. Climb one or two pitches to a snow ledge beneath a steep wall. Traverse right on steep snow to join the crest of Tower Ridge.

The Tower Ridge   600m - 1½kms in length   Grade III***
J.N.Collie, G.A.Solly and J.Collier   29th March 1894
This, the most famous of the great Nevis ridges, is a magnificent expedition. Technically easier than the North East Buttress or Observatory Ridge, it should not be underrated. The main difficulties are concentrated high up and the whole route is exceptionally long and arduous.

The normal winter route avoids the face of the Douglas Boulder by entering the foot of Observatory Gully to the left and then cutting back right to climb the East Gully to Douglas Gap (I). An alternative start is via the Douglas Gap West Gully (I). From the gap a 20m groove/chimney leads to the crest of the ridge which rises gently and becomes quite narrow. It is possible to reach this section and avoid the moves out of the Douglas Gap by traversing in from higher up Observatory Gully over rocky steps and steep snowfields (II). From the narrow section most teams go out right and up beneath steep rocks till overlooking the steep West Flank above Vanishing Gully. Cut back up left and follow the ridge to beneath the Little Tower, very exposed on all sides. The Little Tower usually requires three or four pitches of climbing, starting on the extreme left edge. After these pitches a short level section is reached before another pitch leads to the foot of the Great Tower. On the left side of the tower a very exposed and steeply banked snow ledge (The Eastern Traverse) is followed horizontally left past a slab corner and round an edge to beneath a huge fallen-block chimney. This chimney may be covered

Approaching Tower Gap in a very exposed position.
Climber: Martin Moran

in snow. Ascend the chimney, steep walls and ledges to the top of the Great Tower with some difficulty. Follow the very narrow and exposed crest towards the Tower Gap, descending slightly. Climb down into the gap (tricky!) and either ascend the far wall or move left to belay beneath an icy slab. Ascend some difficult moves via slabs, ledges and chimneys until the angle eases. Climb the final section of the ridge to the plateau, moving right beneath a steep wall at the top. N.B. It is possible to continue the Eastern Traverse by a delicate step further left from the foot of the chimney. This leads to steeply banked snowfields traversing to Tower Gully and avoids the difficulties higher up. This may be a good ploy for teams who are late and tired and wishing to avoid a night out. On reaching Tower Gully it is also possible to descend with care to the hut by a traverse beneath Gardyloo Buttress and on down Observatory Gully.

CLIMBS ON THE DOUGLAS BOULDER
This large area of rock is the lower termination of Tower Ridge and lies immediately above the hut. It is triangular in shape.

Direct Route   215m   Grade IV
Start at the lowest rocks left of an obvious smooth slab. Follow a shallow groove (45m) to an open chimney. Follow this (60m) to a good ledge. Traverse right and climb steeply to the top of the Boulder. N.B. Could be very difficult in lean conditions.

Left-Hand Chimney   215m   Grade IV
R.Carrington and J.R.Marshall   February 1972
Three chimneys in the shape of an inverted 'N' are a feature of the N.W. Face of the Boulder when seen from the hut. This route climbs the left-hand chimney. Start from the left and traverse over snow from the lowest rocks. Gain the chimney by a short vertical wall and follow it with sustained difficulties to the top.

Gutless   180m   Grade IV
P.McKenna and D.Sanderson   March 1979
Some 30m left of the South-West Ridge (left of West Gully) a corner can be seen (Cutlass - summer VS). Left of that corner is a prominent chimney which is climbed to a rightward sloping ledge (90m). Climb

ledge to the edge of the buttress and on to the top of the Boulder.

South West Ridge   180m   Grade III
J.Y.McDonald and H.W.Turnbull   March 1934
Follow the crest of the ridge bounding the left side of Douglas Gap Gully West.

Douglas Gap West Gully   180m   Grade I
A straightforward ascent on steep snow, better scenery than the East Gully. A good low level outing is the combination of Douglas Gap West Gully, followed by the descent of the Douglas Gap East Gully.

CLIMBS FROM COIRE NA CISTE
From the C.I.C. Hut there are several approach routes into Coire na Ciste. The time taken to the higher routes can be as much as an hour. Two hundred metres south-west of the C.I.C. Hut is a steep rocky bluff with deep gorges on its left and right-hand sides. The left-hand gorge has been the scene of some fatal avalanche accidents over the years. Debris appears from the Garadh Buttress area and as far afield as No.2 Gully and Comb Gully! When approaching routes on the left (south) side of the corrie it is best to skirt this gorge on the right where it looks easiest and traverse in high above the gorge beneath Garadh Buttress. Initial difficulties soon ease. Vanishing Gully area can be approached by moving in from close beneath the Douglas Boulder, well above the gorge on its left. The most straightforward approach into Coire na Ciste is by the slopes right (N.W.) of the right-hand gorge mentioned above, or the gorge itself if it has a good banking of snow.

The major feature of Coire na Ciste when seen from the hut are from left to right: Tower Ridge and Secondary Tower Ridge, Garadh Gully and Buttress (Garadh na Ciste) the thin gullies of No.2 and Comb (exits unseen), the triangle of Comb Buttress, the obvious gap of No.3 Gully (lowest point on the skyline), Creag Coire na Ciste, the Trident Buttress area and low down to the left of No.5 Gully is Moonlight Gully Buttress.

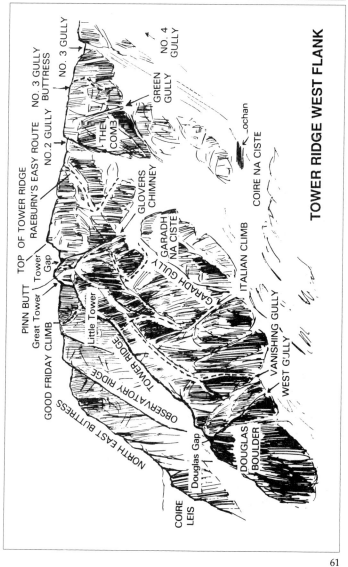

TOWER RIDGE WEST FLANK

NO. 4 GULLY

NO. 3 GULLY
NO. 3 GULLY BUTTRESS
RAEBURN'S EASY ROUTE
NO. 3 GULLY
TOP OF TOWER RIDGE
NO.2 GULLY

GREEN GULLY

THE COMB

lochan

COIRE NA CISTE

GLOVERS CHIMNEY

PINN BUTT
Great Tower
Tower Gap

GARADH NA CISTE

GARADH GULLY

ITALIAN CLIMB

Little Tower

GOOD FRIDAY CLIMB

TOWER RIDGE

OBSERVATORY RIDGE

VANISHING GULLY

WEST GULLY

NORTH EAST BUTTRESS

Douglas Gap

DOUGLAS BOULDER

COIRE LEIS

61

Faulty Towers   155m   Grade II
T.McAulay and N.Muir   2nd April 1980
Take the first icefall right of Douglas Gap West Gully and follow
slightly rightwards to the first narrow crest of Tower Ridge.

1934 Route   185m   Grade II
J.Y.MacDonald and H.W.Turnbull   March 1934
Start 45m right of Douglas Gap West Gully, further right again than
Faulty Towers. Climb via grooves and snow bays to Tower Ridge.

Vanishing Gully   200m   Grade IV/V***
R.Marshall and G.Tiso   15th January 1961
Start at an icefall about 100m right of Douglas Gap West Gully and
climb to a cave with poor belays. Climb out of the cave on very steep
ice and continue until easier ground leads right to Tower Ridge. It is
quicker to descend the ridge from this point rather than carry on up.
N.B. The cave belay is often blocked out by ice.

The Italian Climb   180m   Grade III/IV
J.Marshall, A.MacCorquodale and G.Ritchie   January 1958
Continuing along beneath the west side of Tower Ridge one comes
to a deep gully bounded on the left by a prominent two-tier rib. Climb
the gully; after a starting pitch easy snow leads to another pitch
giving access to a huge recess. Traverse right and ascend an easy
snow slope (frequent avalanche danger) to Tower Ridge.

Italian Climb - Right-Hand   65m   Grade IV**
S Belk and I.Fulton
A popular variation which takes the obvious icefall above the start of
the first pitch and parallel and right of the main gully. The icefall is
long and a poor belay must be taken before the upper snow slope is
reached.

The Chute   230m   Grade IV**
J.R.Marshall, R.N.Campbell and R.Holt   February 1965
About 40m right of Italian Climb this route does not often come into
condition, but when it does an excellent route is the result. Climb by
an extremely steep entry pitch, left then right into a groove which is

followed to a ledge (45m) which leads across a steep wall into a small gully (35m). Traverse up right to beneath a steep ice wall (35m). Climb the ice (25m) and the gully beyond (65m) to the base of a steep buttress. Move easily right into Broad Gully, which can be descended to the corrie or ascended to Tower Ridge.

Garadh Gully   95m   Grade II/III or I !!
I.Clough and M.Burke   16th February 1958
Starts just above and right of Italian Climb and separates the steep little buttress of Garadh na Ciste from Tower Ridge. Can be difficult early in the season, but easy later on. (Easily seen from C.I.C. Hut.)

Garadh Buttress   95m   Grade III
N.Muir and G.Whitten   February 1970
Climb the buttress right of Garadh Gully by a line of snow and ice ramps up its centre.

Broad Gully   95m   Grade II
I.S.Clough and M.Bucke   16th February 1958
From the top of Garadh Gully follow the line of least resistance up leftwards skirting the large buttress above (Pinnacle Buttress) to the crest of Tower Ridge.

To the right of the Garadh and above the exit of the gorge approach, a long snow slope tapers up between the flanks of Tower Ridge and the prominent conical buttress of The Comb, to terminate as No.2 Gully. This slope is the approach for the next climbs.

Pinnacle Buttress of the Tower   150m   Grade III/IV
D.J.Bennett and A.Tait   17th November 1957
Starting from the top of Garadh na Ciste, Broad Gully is followed to the left for about 50m before traversing right along a ledge above overhanging rocks and beneath the steep crest of the buttress. Beyond the crest the rocks are more broken, and the climb now follows a series of snow grooves in the right flank until it is possible to move leftwards to the top of the buttress. Follow a ridge to the foot of the Great Tower and traverse right until a line of chimneys can be followed to the top of it.

Pinnacle Buttress   140m   Grade IV
R.Carrington and B.Hall   March 1976
Start as for Glover's Chimney and climb the icefall to the left of that route to easier ground on the left of the Chimney. Take either of the chimneys above and continue to the top of the Great Tower.

Glover's Chimney   140m   Grade III/IV**
G.G.MacPhee, G.C.Williams and D.Henderson   17th March 1935
Starts above Garadh na Ciste and follows a long couloir leading to a chimney below the Tower Gap. The entry is made by an icefall, often over 35m high and very steep, usually climbed from left to right. The final chimney is the crux. The climb finishes in the Tower Gap. It is possible to descend into Observatory Gully and climb another route if time allows.

The White Line   275m   Grade III**
M.Geddes and H.Gillespie   18th March 1971
Climb the icefall as for Glover's Chimney and continue to the right of the Chimney to a rightward slanting snow ledge. Climb an icefall to a snowfield. Above the snowfield climb a chimney and gully to finish at the top of Tower Ridge.
N.B. All but the initial icefall was originally climbed by T.E.Goodeve, C.Inglis-Clark and J.H.A.McIntyre on 28th December 1907, on an epic escape from Tower Ridge!

Raeburn's Easy Route   110m   Grade II/III*
S.M.C. party   April 1920
The most obvious feature to the right of Glover's Chimney is the deep slit of No.2 Gully with The Comb to its right. To the left of No.2 Gully is No.2 Gully Buttress and to the left again an indefinite wall up which this route winds. Make a long traverse leftwards out of No.2 Gully, across a snow slope and aiming for a point where the crags peter out. Climb a low angled ice pitch then follow a snow shelf back right until a shallow gully gives access to the plateau midway between Tower Ridge and No.2 Gully.

Shot in the dark (IV), Ben Nevis.   Climber: Mark Seaton

Rip Off   120m   Grade IV
P.Braithwaite and J.Lowe   March 1976
This route climbs the steep slabs and walls left of No.2 Gully Buttress.
The most obvious feature is a diagonal fault running across the walls.
Start right of this fault. Follow steep grooves and traverse left onto
steep slabs after 45m. Climb the slabs with little protection for 75m!

Five Finger Discount   135m   Grade IV
M.G.Geddes and C.Higgins   4th February 1978
In the corner between the slabby face of Raeburn's Easy Route and
No.2 Gully Buttress there is a deep groove, defining the left edge of
the buttress. This groove is followed by Rip Off for 30m. Climb the
groove till it bends left and steepens. Move left up an edge to a small
gully and the finish.

Burrito's Groove   135m   Grade IV*
M.G.Geddes and C.Higgins   8th April 1978
Between Five Finger Discount and No.2 Gully Buttress route is a
distinct groove leading directly up the buttress, well seen from below
Comb Buttress. Climb the groove passing an overhang on the left
(45m). Often in condition.

The slopes running up to all of the routes in this area of Ben Nevis are
prone to serious avalanche risk after periods of strong winds and/or
heavy snowfall.

No.2 Gully Buttress   120m   Grade II/III**
J.R.Marshall, L.S.Lovat and A.H.Hendry   23rd March 1958
Immediately to the left of No.2 Gully. Steep snow and occasionally
iced rocks lead to a shelf below a vertical upper wall. A short but
difficult ice pitch on the left leads to easier ground.

No.2 Gully
Left of the obvious triangle of the Comb Buttress a narrow gully can
be seen from the C.I.C. Hut (if weather allows) disappearing up left
into steep rocks. Do not mistake Comb Gully for No.2 Gully. Comb
Gully is very close on the left side of the buttress.

*Climbers John Taylor and Tom Whittaker on the first pitch of
Waterfall Gully (III/IV), Ben Nevis.*

No.2 Gully   120m   Grade I/II**
J.Collier, G.Hastings and W.C.Slingsby   Easter 1896
Hardest and possibly the most interesting of the easier gullies. Above the introductory slopes it becomes a deep slit. Generally a straightforward but steadily steepening slope, it can (especially early in the season) offer an ice pitch and the cornice is often quite difficult. Usually turned on the left.

Comb Gully Buttress   125m   Grade III/IV
I.S.Clough and J.M.Alexander   January 1960
Immediately right of No.2 Gully is Comb Gully Buttress, with Comb Gully on its right side. Climb from just left of the lowest rocks to gain the central snowfield. Entry can also be made from No.2 Gully. Grooves on the left side of the snowfield lead up and right to the foot of a prominent curving chimney which is followed with a difficult exit to the left.
N.B. The chimney above is not often in condition and the following Variation is a better option and gives good climbing.

Variation   75m   Grade IV**
I.Fulton and D.Gardner   January 1971
After the grooves of Comb Gully Buttress on the left side of the buttress traverse left to ice column which is climbed to ice-filled grooves and easy ground.

Comb Gully   125m   Grade III/IV**
F.G.Stangle, R.Morsley and P.A.Small   12th April 1938
The obvious gully running up the left side of The Comb. Easy snow leads to the narrows from where a long pitch leads to a poor belay. Above is a short, steep wall which often gives the crux. Easy ground then leads to the top.

The Comb - Left Flank   100m   Grade IV
G.E.Little and R.Richardson   21st February 1981
Starts 20 metres above Hesperides Ledge. Follow ramp up right to belay below obvious icefall. Climb the icefall and shallow gully to a belay and then on to the top.

Hesperides Ledge   75m   Grade III*
J.R.Marshall, J.Stenhouse and D.Haston   12th February 1959
Follows the lower 75m of Comb Gully and then a relatively easy but highly spectacular steep curving shelf which leads rightwards across the wall to the crest of The Comb.

Tower Face of Comb   215m   Grade V
R.Smith and R.Holt   January 1959
A difficult and sustained mixed climb which receives very few ascents. A large ledge splits the buttress diagonally at one-third height from left to right. From the bottom left end of this ledge move up to another ledge running parallel to the lower ledge (30m). Go right to the foot of an obvious groove (25m). Climb the groove, going left to easier climbing and the base of a steep wall (50m). Traverse right by walls and steep snow to the buttress crest. The easier ground above can be difficult in strong winds and deep snow.

Pigott's Route   245m   Grade IV
J.Marshall and R.Smith   12th February 1960
From the C.I.C. Hut an obvious large ramp/ledge can be seen cutting up from left to right across the bottom section of the triangle of Comb Buttress. Follow this ramp up right till beneath a chimney (35m left of Green Gully). Climb the chimney (hard) and traverse left into steep ice-filled grooves which are followed to the buttress crest.

Mercury   150m   Grade V
M.Hind and J.Christie   26th January 1985
Ascends the right-most of four parallel grooves just left of Green Gully. Climb Green Gully for 10m and move left around a rib to belay beneath a chimney with a chockstone (20m, might be possible to climb direct). Climb up and traverse left (loose) past a small overhang to the main groove line on the left (30m crux). Continue up more easily to the crest of the buttress.

Green Gully   180m   Grade III/IV***
H.Raeburn and E.Phildius   April 1906
A classic. The obvious gully running up the right side of Comb Buttress.

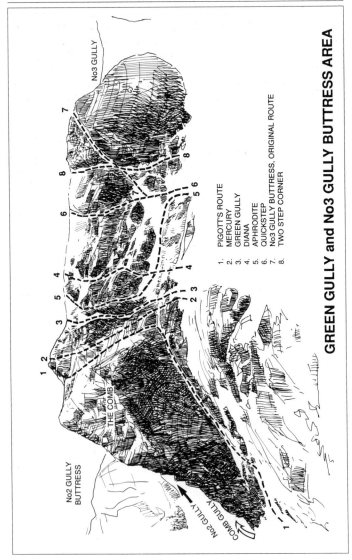

No3 GULLY

7

8

8

6

5 6

4

5

3

2 3

1 2

THE COMB

No2 GULLY
BUTTRESS

No2 GULLY

COMB GULLY

1. PIGOTT'S ROUTE
2. MERCURY
3. GREEN GULLY
4. DIANA
5. APHRODITE
6. QUICKSTEP
7. No3 GULLY BUTTRESS, ORIGINAL ROUTE
8. TWO STEP CORNER

GREEN GULLY and No3 GULLY BUTTRESS AREA

The first pitch changes in character from steep ice to a Grade I/II snow slope depending on build-up. Good peg belays on the left wall after 45m. Above are normally two or three good ice pitches with belays on the right side of the gully wall. When the gully opens out to a steep snow slope near the top three exits present themselves. By easy snow to the right, a fine direct ice pitch (**) or a traverse left to the ridge. If the cornice presents a problem, one of these finishes should fix it!

No.3 Gully Buttress is the name given to the steep cliffs extending right from Green Gully to No.3 Gully. The very steep rocks at the left-hand side of the mouth of No.3 Gully have a snow bay on their left which gives access to the Original Route and others in this area. Alternative starts are described in the route details. Being high up the hill this area should provide good climbing, but be careful of the mean-looking cornices.

Venus 190m Grade IV
M.Duff and A.Nisbet 28th January 1982
Follows the arête which forms the right bank of Green Gully. At half-height it is possible to move into grooves on the right and then back onto the arête higher up. The stances are poor and a long rope (60m!) is recommended to avoid them. Avoiding moves are often possible to the right, making this a fairly artificial line. The top section of this climb is common with Aphrodite, described next.

Aphrodite 200m Grade III/IV
M.G.Geddes and J.C.Higham 15th March 1971
Start up the same snow depression as Original Route (described later). Move a long way left at the top over snowfields and ledges, then down to the foot of an open groove. This groove is beside a rib right of Green Gully and is undercut by a large rock wall. Climb the groove and then the arête beside Green Gully, moving right at the top to a cornice which can be huge.

Diana 195m Grade V
M.Duff and J.Tinker 16th February 1985
Start at the obvious icefall 30m left of the snow depression of No.3

Gully Buttress Original Route. Climb the icefall direct past a horizontal snow band to belay beneath a steep rock wall, (55m). On the left climb a groove/chimney past a roof/chockstone to another snow band and huge block stance (45m). Follow corners to beneath a huge right-facing corner (30m). Up to the overlap and pull onto the right wall of the corner then straight up on steep thin ice to easier ground (45m). Follow snow to possible large cornice finish.

Quickstep   130m   Grade IV**
R.Townsend and T.Bray   26th March 1983
The huge leftward facing corner with steep slabs on its left, directly above the start of the Original Route. Climb the Original Route to the traverse ledge, then continue up to the foot of the corner. Steep ice on the left of the corner to belay at 45m. The final pitch leads to a conical basin above, which is often overhung by massive cornices which may be passable to the right by exposed and steep climbing.

No.3 Gully Buttress Original Route   125m   Grade III**
L.S.Lovat and D.J.Bennet   18th February 1957
Climb up into the large snow bay below the prow of the buttress. From the top of the bay exit right to a platform, then follow grooves leftwards to a steep corner finish or traverse up rightwards. The upper part of the route is magnificently exposed.

Two-Step Corner   130m   Grade IV**
D.Kirtley and D.Montgomery   March 1975
Starts 20m to the right of the Original Route and follows a corner to the traverse ledge of that route. Climb directly up the steep corner above to a difficult cornice exit.

Thompson's Route   120m   III/IV*
R.Marshall, J.R.Marshall and J.Stenhouse   December 1963
Immediately on the right of the very steep front face of the buttress at the bottom left of No.3 Gully, is a chimney. Follow this steeply and with interest to join the Original Route at the platform.

No.3 Gully   150m   Grade I*
The lowest point in the skyline looking S.W. from the C.I.C. Hut. First

ascent dates back to pre-1870. The angle of the approach slope gradually increases as it rises from the basin of Coire na Ciste and by the time it narrows to a gully proper, it is quite steep. No pitches but the final section is divided by a pinnacle rib. The exit will be dictated by the cornice.

South Gully, Creag Coire na Ciste   125m   Grade II/III
G.G.MacPhee   10th April 1936
Starts high up on the left-hand side of Creag Coire na Ciste and just below No.3 Gully proper. Use an obvious ramp slanting diagonally to the right. This leads to an ice pitch which gives entry to a final steep funnel. Cornice is often difficult.

Central Gully   125m   Grade III
I.Clough and J.M.Alexander   27th January 1959
Starting from the lowest part of the crag, snow slopes are followed to the left of a rocky rib to reach the left-hand of two parallel ice chimneys which cleave the steep central wall. This is climbed for 40m before crossing to the right-hand gully which leads into the final corniced funnel.

Central Gully - Right-Hand   125m   Grade IV**
I.MacEacheron and J.Knight
The right-hand chimney gives a fine long pitch. An independent start can be made by climbing the rightward slanting icefall to the left of North Gully then traversing left to the foot of the chimney.

North Gully   110m   Grade II
J.Y.MacDonald and H.W.Turnbull   24th March 1934
The right-hand and most obvious of the three gullies on this cliff, starts to the left of No.4 Gully. The lower section of the gully almost always holds an ice pitch but its length may vary from 3m to 30m. The narrow lower section leads to a wide easier angled slope which is followed obliquely rightwards to the cornice. Beware of avalanche danger on the final slopes.

No.4 Gully   150m   Grade I
The easiest winter route on Ben Nevis and the best descent on the

North Face. It curls gently round to the right between the cliffs of Creag Coire na Ciste and the South Trident Buttress. Its exit is very wide so that, even given a heavy build-up of cornice, it should be possible to find an easy weakness. This route cannot be seen from the C.I.C. Hut.

The area which extends from No.4 Gully on the left to No.5 Gully on the right contains the Trident Buttress group (South, Central and North) whose crests can be seen cutting the skyline. The following routes are located on these rocks, starting from Lochan na Ciste (GR 162718).

Joyful Chimneys   180m   Grade III
R.Campbell, J.R.Marshall   February 1971
A discontinuous line of chimneys can be seen on the flank of South Trident Buttress facing the C.I.C. Hut. Starts 50m left and downhill of Central Gully (described next). These chimneys are either climbed or avoided on their flanks, depending on conditions. The crest of South Trident Buttress is gained by a series of grooves above the chimneys.

Central Gully   240m   Grade III
H.Raeburn and Mr & Mrs C. Inglis-Clark   April 1904
Immediately above (west) of the small lochans (Lochan Coire na Ciste) and right of the steep rocks of South Trident Buttress. This gully can fill up almost completely. Often a steep ice column is found barring the way. Either pass it by mixed ground up to the left (as on the first ascent) or climb direct. Above a variety of routes lead to the top avoiding difficulties as necessary.

Jubilee Climb   240m   Grade II
G.G.MacPhee, G.C.Williams and D.Henderson   May 1935
In the lower part of Central Gully is a rightward leading branch which is followed on snow and small ice pitches to easy ground and a choice of routes to the top.

Jubilation   240m   Grade III*
R.Marshall, J.R.Marshall and J.Stenhouse   December 1963
Follow Jubilee Climb for about 75m. Traverse left into a chimney and climb it on steep ice to a snow bay. Move left into a second chimney

and follow this until it eases. A choice of routes lead over easier ground to the top.

Neptune Gully 160m Grade III
A.J.Bennet and J.Clarkson February 1956
This S-shaped gully splits the crest of the North Trident (right-hand) Buttress. It has an indefinite entry pitch 10 metres to the left of the upper section of Moonlight Gully (described next) from the large flat ledge. Climb first on the right and enter the gully higher up which is followed turning ice pitches on the left to a large platform overlooking No.5 Gully. Ascend an easy ridge and slopes above to the plateau.

At the bottom of No.5 Gully on the left is Moonlight Gully Buttress which is split at two-thirds height by a very large (almost flat) ledge. At such a low altitude the climbs will not be in good condition so often, but offer alternatives when the weather high up is bad.

Moonlight Gully 150m Grade I/II
W.Inglis-Clark and T.Gibson January 1908
This gully is on the immediate left of Moonlight Gully Buttress and provides a steep and narrow snow climb which ends in the upper area of No.5 Gully.

Diagonal Route 150m Grade II
D.Hawthorn, C.MacLean and A.Paul 17th January 1983
Start at the foot of Moonlight Gully. Traverse up right to a broad ledge and continue by the left-hand chimney above to the big ledge. Climb the upper tier by the continuation of the chimney.

Right-Hand Chimney 135m Grade III
D.Hawthorn, C.MacLean and A.Paul 17th December 1983
Two chimneys split the front face of the buttress. The right-hand one is better defined and is climbed direct and its continuation followed on the second tier above the big ledge, sustained.

Phosphorescent Grooves 175m Grade III/IV
K.V.Crocket, A.Walker and R.T.Richardson 22nd December 1985
A traverse line up the face overlooking No.5 Gully. Start just left of

the gully entrance and climb easily to a large ledge. Up a steep wall and right to belay on a large ledge by a slab corner. Climb the corner to a belay and go right into an awkward 5m chimney, which is climbed to another belay. Descend a little then up to the large ledge above.

No.5 Gully   460m   Grade I*
Collie and party   April 1895

Obvious from the C.I.C. Hut. Prone to very large avalanches. Lies between the Trident Buttresses and the Great Buttress of Carn Dearg and commences below and well to the right of the main basin of Coire na Ciste. It is a straightforward snow climb. Above a small pitch the gully narrows, and then opens into a huge funnel. The normal route keeps to the right, to exit near the top of Carn Dearg N.W.

Ledge Route   450m   Grade II***

The best on the mountain at this grade. A very interesting excursion. Starts up No.5 Gully but leaves it by a rightwards rising ramp shortly after it becomes a gully proper. The ramp leads out above the top of The Curtain onto a broad, almost horizontal ledge which fades out to the right. Before the ledge narrows, leave it by a leftward slanting gully which comes out onto a broad sloping snow shelf. This shelf gives an easier but less interesting start; it comes out of No.5 Gully and slants easily up to the right to a large platform at the summit of the Great Buttress of Carn Dearg. A large pinnacle block, a useful landmark, is passed just before rounding the corner to reach the platform. The route now follows the ridge and is in places very narrow. A further connecting ridge leads on up to the summit of Carn Dearg N.W. In good weather this route gives a more interesting, if slower, descent than the gullies.

In Descent

The ridge should be followed down to the top of Carn Dearg Buttress and then the broad highest shelf (marked by the pinnacle block at the start) can be followed easily into No.5 Gully. Instead of descending the gully (which may have a small pitch in it), continue to the far side where a similar broad shelf leads gradually down from the large ledge at the top of Moonlight Gully Buttress, towards Lochan na Ciste. This descent passage also provides a good approach if avalanches are possible in No.5 Gully.

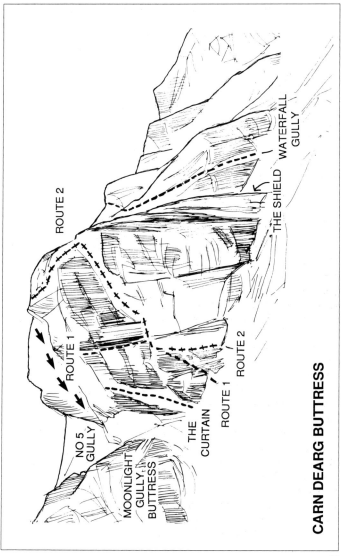

ROUTE 2

ROUTE 1

NO 5 GULLY

MOONLIGHT GULLY BUTTRESS

THE CURTAIN

ROUTE 1

ROUTE 2

THE SHIELD

WATERFALL GULLY

CARN DEARG BUTTRESS

CARN DEARG BUTTRESS

The great buttress of Carn Dearg lies to the right of No. 5 Gully and contains some of the most difficult winter climbs in Scotland.

The Curtain Rail   80m   Grade IV
D.F.Lang, R.T.Richardson and C.Stead   31st January 1988 (first recorded ascent!)
Follows the grooves left of and parallel to The Curtain (described next) and can provide an interesting alternative to that overcrowded climb.

The Curtain   110m   Grade IV/V***
J.Knight and D.Bathgate   February 1965
Climbed more times than any other ice route in Britain.

On the left side of Carn Dearg Buttress immediately right of No.5 Gully, and a definite candidate for a multiple pile-up. One day a climber will fall from the top pitch and wipe out all the ropes below. Absurd tactics have been seen on this route, with two separate parties climbing in parallel on all of the three pitches. If you value your life, try and climb the route on a quiet day which is not often possible. For people staying in the hut, they should be able to ascend the route either before or after the hordes have arrived or descended!

A 50m rope is useful to gain the cave belay on the first pitch and to reach the rocks after the last pitch. Climb the long slab to a belay on the right 45m. Zig-zag up the next pitch to belay on the left wall. Traverse right and climb the final steep ice wall and slab.

N.B. If the belayer lets the ropes hang down the second pitch, they can easily get caught under the icicle fringe. Descent is made into No.5 Gully by a steep snow slope on the left after the final difficulties.

P.M.   110m   Grade IV/V
B.Hall and A.Rouse   10th February 1986
From the foot of The Curtain an obvious ledge runs right above very steep ground to a large deep chimney (Route I, described next) after approximately 60m. This line follows a corner (turf) to the left of the chimney for two pitches then crosses the chimney for an exciting finish on the right.

N.B. Climbed in good conditions on the first ascent, this route may vary in difficulty considerably. Also it appears that this route was climbed in 1985 by Mal Duff and J.Tinker using the direct start of Route II, following the turf line mentioned on P.M. and finishing up Route I, instead of crossing that climb as did Hall/Rouse. They called their climb Sod's Law 300m Grade V/VI.

Route I   215m   Grade V/VI
D.Knowles and D.Wilson   1972

An obvious ledge runs right from the foot of The Curtain. After about 60m it arrives at the bottom of a large obvious chimney. This chimney gives the top half of the climb and can be very hard. It is possible to take a more direct start by climbing the minor buttress below and to the right of The Curtain and traversing the ledge mentioned above to the foot of the chimney section. The Direct starts from just left of the lowest rocks of the minor buttress and climbs via ledges and cracks to a big block belay at 45m. From here, go left and climb grooves to the traverse ledge at the top of the minor buttress.

Route II   150m   V/VI**
M.Geddes and A.Rouse   12th February 1978

Climb the first pitch of the chimney of Route I (20m). Then follow an upward diagonal line across the slabs, beneath the overhangs, rightwards to a groove line at the far edge of the buttress. Follow this groove line up the crest to easy ground. A superb climb in an exciting situation, not often in condition. Three pegs were used for tension on the first ascent.

Route II Direct   75m   VI***
G.Smith and I.Sykes   15th February 1978

Starts in a deep corner at the lowest point of rocks right of Route I Direct start. Climb the corner and traverse left beneath an overhang. Climb up to a large block and climb a groove above it. Traverse right round an arête to a ledge and climb bulge above to the traverse ledge. Follow the Geddes/Rouse route to the top. Combined with the original Route II climb (Geddes/Rouse), the Direct provides a high quality route of considerable difficulty when in condition.

The Shadow   245m   Grade VI**
P.Braithwaite and D.Pearce   March 1979

Starts 10m right of Route II Direct. Follow a crack-line and groove to belay (20m). Traverse right, continuing to an obvious line of overhangs beneath the traverse line of Route II. Continue this traverse right to the junction with Centurion, which is gained with difficulty (40m). Continue across Centurion and up right to below large overhang (20m). Climb exposed broken crack-line through right side of overhangs to snowy recess on arête (15m). Climb overhanging groove until a difficult move left can be made onto icy rib. Climb rib with difficulty, then move slightly left to join Sassenach and follow grooves above to finish.

Shield Direct   290m   Grade VI**
M.Fowler and A.Saunders   March 1979

The first recorded Grade VI on the mountain, a soaring line of great difficulty. A long way right of the previous climbs the front face of Carn Dearg Buttress turns to form a vertical line of cliffs facing north. Waterfall Gully (described later) is an obvious feature to the right. On the vertical wall is a series of steep chimneys, which give the line of the route. Start in a steep icy groove (often blank), directly below the chimney line. Follow the groove to a stance at 24m. Climb steeply to a large ledge on the right at the foot of the chimney. Climb the difficult chimney to a cave (30m). Steep ice grooves lead to easier climbing at the top of the chimney flake (75m). Move left past a flake and bulges to trend right by easiest line to ledges (45m). Climb up right then left to easier ground, followed by an arête to the junction with Ledge Route.

Gemini   300m   Grade V**
A.Paul and D.Sanderson   23rd March 1979

Climb the first two pitches of Waterfall Gully (described next). Above on the left wall a series of rightward sloping ice ramps and steep ice smears sometimes form. These are followed to an enormous detached flake. Climb very steep ice on the wall left of the flake to a ledge and rightward sloping grooves. Move up and right to obvious twin grooves, either of which can be climbed to a broad ledge which is followed right. Climb up via iced slabs to easier ground.

A very steep direct start to the left of the first pitch of Waterfall Gully can be climbed, thus avoiding that route entirely. (A.McIntyre and A.Kimber 1st April 1979. V.**)

Waterfall Gully   215m   Grade III/IV*
D.Pipes, I.Clough, J.Alexander, R.Shaw and A.Flegg   8th January 1959
The obvious gully immediately right of Carn Dearg Buttress.

After the first steep 45m the angle eases and leads with a rightwards traverse after 150m to the large basin below the summit buttresses.

A direct finish to Waterfall Gully is possible by continuing straight up where the gully swings right onto the ridge. (D.Cuthbertson and C.Fraser 1984. V.)

High up above and to the right of Waterfall Gully is a large hanging snow corrie. At its bottom lip an overhung icefall can often be seen from the approach to the C.I.C. Hut. To the right of this icefall is an obvious snow/ice gully which gives the start to some of the following routes. Access to these climbs can be made from below the hut over the steep and rocky ground beneath The Castle. Please be aware that many avalanche fatalities have occurred in this area over the years. This approach is exposed to these dangers for most of its length. A far safer approach is to ascend from the hut to beneath the Carn Dearg Buttress and traverse below it towards the climbs.

Descent from the large hanging snow corrie is easiest by Ledge Route, which is gained by ascending the steep slopes on the left side of the corrie to the ridge above.

Harrison's Climb Direct   300m   Grade III/IV*
C.G.M.Slessor and N.Tennant   1961
Beneath the overhung icefall and slightly right is a detached buttress not easily recognised on the approach (Cousins Buttress). This climb ascends a steep icy chimney at its left side. Move up the chimney and rightwards until the top of the buttress is reached. From the saddle at the back of the buttress gain the wall beyond and move up and left by a long rising traverse into the large hanging snow corrie from which a variety of exits are possible.
N.B. The hanging snow corrie often releases large avalanches, so be wary after strong winds and/or heavy snow falls.

North East Face Route (Cousins Buttress Ordinary Route) 275m
III/IV*
H.Brunton and J.Clarkson 14th February 1957
Follow the obvious snow/ice gully mentioned in the approach
details previously, climbing one short ice pitch. Move left from below
an ice-fall to the top of the buttress (Cousins) mentioned in Harrison's
Direct. Follow a ledge left and climb the right side of a large exposed
ice-fall to the corrie above. A variety of exits are possible.

Raeburn's Buttress/Intermediate Gully 230m Grade III/IV**
W.D.Brooker and J.M.Taylor (by the buttress finish).
R.H.Sellers and J.Smith (finishing by Intermediate Gully). 31st January 1959
G.G.MacPhee and party had previously made a first ascent of the gully in
April 1938, but perhaps not under true winter conditions.
Raeburn's is the tall thin buttress above the left-hand corner of the
Castle Corrie. It finishes as a slender tapering arête to the left of which
is the prominent narrow Intermediate Gully. The start is the same as
for North East Face Route; the gully leading up into the left-hand
corner of the corrie. After about 65m an obvious chimney line on the
right leads up to a cave (the impressive icefall of the left branch is
Boomer's Requiem, described next) and then the route takes the right
wall to reach the foot of Intermediate Gully. There is a cave exit at the
top of the gully which is otherwise straightforward. The crest of
Raeburn's Buttress proper is immediately to the right of the foot of
the gully. It narrows to a sharp blade at the top but this may be turned
by a corner on the right.

Boomer's Requiem 170m Grade IV (very steep!)
C.Higgins and D.MacArthur February 1973
Above the first gully on Raeburn's Buttress is an obvious icefall
leading to a snow patch. Climb the icefall and up another ice pitch
above the snow patch to beneath the summit gullies.

Raeburn's Buttress (III/IV), Ben Nevis. Climber: Alan Kimber

CARN DEARG SUMMIT GULLIES

These form a logical continuation to some of the previous climbs. They may also be reached by descending into the basin from high up on Ledge Route. Climbed by I.Clough, P.S.Nicholson and D.Pipes 8th & 12th April 1958.

Colando Gully   105m   Grade I   *8th April 1958*
The left-hand gully. Straightforward.

Arch Buttress   185m   Grade II/III
D.Pipes and A.Flegg   3rd January 1959
Between Arch and Colando gullies. After 45m on the crest, the route follows a groove on the right then easier climbing to some difficult chimneys.

Arch Gully   105m   Grade I   *8th April 1958*
The central gully marked by a huge block which forms the Arch at about half-height. Straightforward but steep.

Surprise Buttress   190m   Grade III
I.Clough and B.Halpin   3rd January 1959
On the buttress to the right of Arch Gully, following the crest as closely as possible to a steep wall above the Arch block. A 33m rightwards traverse below this wall is followed by short awkward walls leading back slightly left to a small ledge about 10m above the traverse. A move downwards and to the right gives entry to a steep 35m corner which gives a strenuous final crux pitch.

Surprise Gully   185m   Grade I/II   *12th April 1958*
The shallow right-hand gully leads by broken rocks to a shoulder and to the top by an ice groove on the left.

The Aonach Eagach Ridge, Glencoe, (II/III). Climbers descending from the difficult step on Am Bodach at the start of the ridge. This is one of the crux sections to the traverse.

CLIMBS FROM CASTLE CORRIE

On the approach up the Allt a'Mhuilinn the first main feature is the North Face of Castle Ridge up on the right, to its left is Castle Ridge. The area to the left of Castle Ridge is known as Castle Corrie and is only seen fully from a point approximately half a kilometre downhill of the hut. The main features are the North and South Castle Gullies which are separated by The Castle at their top, and join at their foot into a steep rocky icefall/gully descending towards the Half Way Lochan approach path. The approaches to the climbs and hazards involved are the same as for the routes to the right of Carn Dearg Buttress.

Compression Crack 130m Grade V
M.Hind and C.Rice 9th February 1985
On the steep wall left of South Castle Gully and below Raeburn's Arête a series of imposing ice smears can often be seen. Climb this ice and traverse a long way right to reach iced cracks. Follow the corner above vertically for 15m and a further 20m to easy ground.

Winter Chimneys 145m Grade IV
I.S.Clough and R.Sefton 28th January 1960
Although little is known about this route it is given as a possible landmark for the previous climb. Go beyond Compression Crack for about 30m to a deep chimney topped by a huge capstone. The capstone was avoided by pegging on the right wall on the first ascent.

CASTLE GULLIES

These two climbs can be anything from straightforward snow ascents, to awkward chockstone-filled trenches depending on the amount of snow. They are also very prone to avalanches after strong winds and/or snowfall.

South Castle Gully 230m Grade I/II*
W.Brunskill, W.W.King and W.W.Naismith 1st April 1896
The long gully between Raeburn's Buttress and The Castle. Normally an easy snow climb. One small pitch may be particularly difficult early in the season; climbed by a gangway on the left wall.

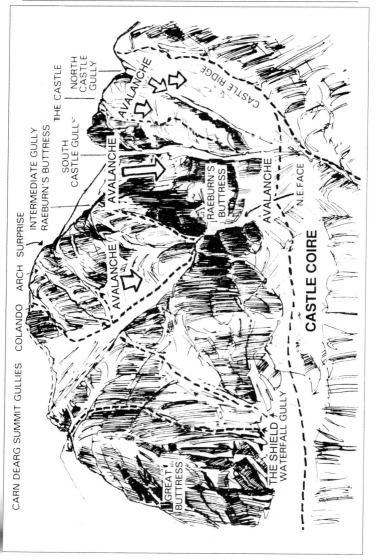

CARN DEARG SUMMIT GULLIES   COLANDO   ARCH   SURPRISE   INTERMEDIATE GULLY   RAEBURN'S BUTTRESS   THE CASTLE   NORTH CASTLE GULLY   CASTLE RIDGE

SOUTH CASTLE GULLY

AVALANCHE

AVALANCHE

AVALANCHE

RAEBURN'S BUTTRESS

AVALANCHE   N.E. FACE

AVALANCHE

CASTLE COIRE

THE SHIELD   WATERFALL GULLY

GREAT BUTTRESS

The Castle   230m   Grade II/III*
W.Brown, J.MacLay, W.W.Naismith and G.Thomson   April 1896
In summer an awkward bulging little wall guards the base. This may be hard in winter but more probably it will be entirely obliterated by an avalanche cone. The route then goes straight up. The upper rocks are climbed by means of a gully, slabs, a chimney and a further shallow gully all in the centre of the buttress, to beneath the final very steep wall. The route now goes up to the right over snow-covered slabs, to the top. Great care should be taken on the slabby sections which are prone to avalanche.

North Castle Gully   230m   Grade I/II*
J.H.Bell and R.G.Napier   4th April 1896
The gully bounding The Castle on the right. Steeper than South Castle Gully, it contains several easy chockstone pitches, often completely covered giving a straightforward snow climb.

Castle Ridge   275m   Grade II (III** at the chimney)
J.N.Collie, W.W.Naismith, G.Thomson and M.W.Traverse   12th April 1895
A fine outing. The easiest of the Nevis Ridges (after Ledge Route) and possible in most conditions. If avalanche conditions prevail it is very difficult (if not impossible) to avoid them on the approaches from beneath, or the traverse from below Carn Dearg Buttress. Start 150m below the point where The Castle Gullies meet and traverse right onto the blunt crest of the ridge by the easiest line. Ascend via ledges, walls and slabs using the easiest line, until the crest is blocked by a band of steep walls. Traverse up and right with difficulty via a flaky chimney in a very exposed position overlooking the North Face to a good ledge and belay. Another difficult pitch leads to an easing in the ridge. Follow more easily to the top of the ridge.
N.B. For teams who are considering descending to the Half Way Lochan (Grid Square 1472) a traverse of the hillside due west (300m) must be made before descending. A number of accidents have occurred in this area with people falling down the North Face, which is immediately on your right at the top of the ridge. In good weather and with enough time, a fine way to round off this ascent is to go up to the north summit of Carn Dearg N.W. (1214m GR 159721) and

descend Ledge Route. Alternatively a bearing heading south-west from that summit will lead into the easy Red Burn descent.

CLIMBS ON THE NORTH FACE OF CASTLE RIDGE

This very extensive, steep and broken area of rock is the first significant part of the climbing areas as seen across the Allt a'Mhuilinn approach on the right. The left edge is Castle Ridge and to its right is an overhanging section of rock with an obvious groove on its right (Lobby Dancer). Large snow terraces traverse the face from bottom left towards the shoulder of Carn Dearg N.W.

The Lobby Dancer 280m Grade V**
C.Higgins and A.Kimber 28th February 1977
The left-hand section of the face is dominated by a clean overhanging wall split by a groove. Come in to the foot of the groove from the left by a diagonal ledge or more directly by ice pitches. Climb the groove for 3 pitches to a barrier from where an escape left is made on aid to another groove. Up this groove and on up to Castle Ridge.

Alchemist 270m Grade V
A.Paul and D.Sanderson 26th March 1979
Start as for Serpent then follow an icefall to the foot of the groove system just right of the main groove of Lobby Dancer. Climb the groove system to the barrier which is crossed by the right wall of a huge flake, on aid, to a narrow ice chimney. Climb the chimney, move left then right to a cave. Go right around the arête and follow the groove to Castle Ridge.

Last Day in Purgatory 330m Grade V
C.Higgins and M.Geddes 8th April 1979
Takes an impressive zig-zag line up ledge systems to the clean face right of The Lobby Dancer.

The Serpent 300m Grade II
I.Clough, D.Pipes and J.Porter 12th February 1959
The easiest of the routes on the North Face of Castle Ridge. No technical difficulty but serious, with route-finding problems. Above and to the left of the Lunching Stone (Glen Nevis approach) a small

right slanting gully gives access to a wide shelf which curves up to the right. After 165m this leads into a couloir which slants rightwards, steeply up the face to come out on the shoulder of Carn Dearg, N.W.

The Moat   500m   Grade II**
I.Sykes, I.Rae and I.Dewar   8th February 1972
A great, highly banked snow ledge runs across the face above The Serpent and gives the line of the climb. Follow The Serpent for 70 metres then move left to gain the ledge. At the end of the ledge finish by a steep gully. A fine outing across this huge face.

Nordwand   425m   Grade II/III*
I.Clough, D.Pipes, B.Sarll, F.Jones and J.Porter   11th February 1959
A fine mixed route. Technical and route-finding problems similar to those on the Little Brenva Face but no sunshine; a genuine, grim nordwand atmosphere. Starts fairly well to the right of the centre of the face at a slight bay. A long vertical snow-filled trench on the screes below the face often shows the way. Nordwand follows a short gully up the face for 30m and climbs an ice pitch before moving left (or works diagonally left below the ice pitch). It continues to follow the easiest way up the centre of the wall crossing the couloir of The Serpent and continuing by snowfields to the steep summit rocks. An awkward left rising traverse leads to the top.

Casino Royale   190m   Grade V
M.Duff, R.Nowack and A.Bond   29th February 1988
Starts at an obvious thin gully just left of La Petite. Climb the walls, snow bays and an icefall to below a roof. Move left with difficulty to a thin ice smear in a corner which is followed to the top. Go rightwards at the top to finish.

La Petite   200m   Grade III
D.Pipes and I.Clough   11th February 1959
The climbs starts about 30m right of Nordwand and goes up steeply for 40m to gain entry to a couloir. This entry will generally give a 25m ice pitch and then ice glazed rock. The couloir, which leads obliquely right (not obvious from below) should give two more good ice pitches before finishing on the Carn Dearg shoulder.

CLIMBS ON STOB BAN (999m) - MAMORES

The North-East face of this steep-sided and rocky peak provides good climbing on ridges; buttresses and gullies when in condition. The shapely summit cone is best seen from Glen Nevis Youth Hostel. An easy approach on a good path is made from the Lower Falls (GR 145684) up the east bank of the Allt Coire a'Mhusgain. Ascend this path to a point opposite the cliffs (GR 155660 - $1^1/_2$ - 2 hours), then descend for a short distance to cross the main stream below the cliffs. Approaching the cliffs from this point allows for a good reconnaissance before choosing the correct line of ascent, as the cliffs are more complicated than they may at first appear.

From this point on the path the features are as follows, left to right: East Wing, South Gully, South (summit) Buttress, North Gully, Central Buttress (this appears as a triangular mass of rock set forward and at a lower level than South Buttress) and a long flat col has North Buttress to its right (see diagram).

The routes recommended are as follows:
South Gully   150m   Grade I*
North Gully   150m   Grade I

There are three gully lines on the left (N.E.) flank of Central Buttress. The right-hand two are close together.

No Toddy   150m   Grade III
D.Hawthorn, R.Lee and D.N.Williams   April 1986
Climbs the left-hand gully. Start at a small snowfield some distance up the left flank of the buttress. Climb a steep ice pitch to easier ground and a stance on the right. Move back left and ascend the gully easily until it slants right. The right slant has been climbed on an earlier ascent by Malcolm Creasey and party, on that ascent the whole climb was graded IV. Traverse left and bridge up a continuation of the lower line. Follow mixed ground to the top of buttress.

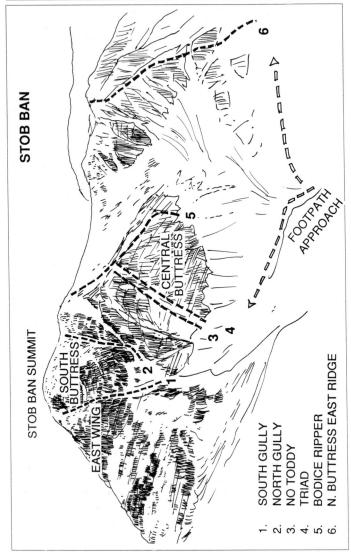

STOB BAN

STOB BAN SUMMIT

SOUTH BUTTRESS

EAST WING

CENTRAL BUTTRESS

FOOTPATH APPROACH

1. SOUTH GULLY
2. NORTH GULLY
3. NO TODDY
4. TRIAD
5. BODICE RIPPER
6. N. BUTTRESS EAST RIDGE

The central gully line (no name) was climbed in 1969 by J.Grieve and C.MacNaughton, Grade IV (for 25m), 150m. Follow the gully and go back left along an easy ramp to gain the crest of the ridge which leads easily to the top of the buttress.

Triad 150m Grade III
D.Hawthorn, R.Lee and D.N.Williams April 1986
Climbs the right-hand gully. Start between two narrow rock buttresses. Ascend the gully which gradually steepens and narrows to a chimney. Reach a stance where the right-hand buttress finishes and a ledge runs across the left-hand buttress. Follow a snow ramp on the right, traverse left along a narrow ledge to the buttress crest. Join the easy leftward slanting ramp above as for the previous route.
N.B. The buttress between these last two routes has been climbed, (Grade IV).

Bodice Ripper 150m Grade IV
J.Murphy and D.N.Williams March 1984
Climbs the large triangular face on the front of Central Buttress. Start right of centre at the foot of an obvious rightward slanting gully. Ascend easily to a prominent leftward slanting ramp. Follow this until it fades and take a poor stance at the foot of a steep and narrow rightward slanting slab. Climb the slab with difficulty to its end and zig-zag up the snow slope above (crux). Continue to the top of the snowfield and ascend the obvious gully. At the top, squeeze up the narrow chimney (Bodice Ripper) leading rightwards. A broad ramp leads left and then by a narrow crest towards the summit.
N.B. A short section of arête at the end of all of the routes on Central Buttress link to the main ridge 200m north of the summit.

North Buttress - East Ridge 200m Grade II/III
Brown, Hinxman, Tough and Douglas Easter 1895
This ridge is best approached from the same direction as all the other routes on Stob Ban, with a traverse across the corrie floor, hard right (NW) beneath Central Buttress. Head up towards the route from a flat spot (GR 151660). An excellent exercise in route-finding with tremendous views down Glen Nevis and a fine arête near the top.

Descent

From the summit two fine airy ridges can be used to descend. The North Ridge is the shortest and descends steeply over two subsidiary summits. After approximately 2kms bear north-west to avoid steep grass and rocky outcrops before arriving back at the start point. Alternatively it is possible to descend the steep East Ridge, taking care to avoid the sharply incut gullies to your left (N.W.) After approximately 1km good paths lead back in a northerly direction towards the original ascent path.

N.B. These two descent ridges can also be used as an interesting method of ascent and should really be graded in their final hundred metres (I).

CLIMBS IN GLEN NEVIS

The following routes are outlined as alternatives for a short day if the weather and conditions (deep freeze for two weeks) allow.

Achintee Gully   200m   Grade II/III
Burns, Newbigging and Raeburn   1904
The obvious deep slit in the hillside above the car park (GR 126730). Requires a fall of snow low down followed by prolonged freezing.

Steall Waterfall   120m   II/III**
I.G.Rowe   1st January 1963
The large waterfall above Steall Hut (GR 177683) can provide good sport, if it freezes enough. Abseil descent using the trees on the left side.

Winter Wall - Polldubh Crags   30m   Grade II/III
As with a number of water weeps on these cliffs a good freeze will bring this climb into condition offering a bit of fun in the valley. Use the Glen Nevis rock climbing guidebook!

AONACH MOR   1221m (GR 193730), and AONACH BEAG   1234m (GR 196715)
Along with Ben Nevis and Carn Mor Dearg, their close neighbours, these two peaks form part of the original quartet of 4,000 Munro

summits that existed in Lochaber before the metric incursion. Until recently they have been reserved for the climber who preferred solitude and long walks. With the development of the Aonach Mor ski slopes by the company of Nevis Range, these peaks will no doubt be subjected to increased interest from climbers with enough brass to catch the Gondola.

Climbing on the flanks of these peaks is varied and interesting. The main areas being the East and West Faces of Aonach Mor and the North - North East and West Faces of Aonach Beag.

Approaches
On foot from the valley!

Aonach Mor West Face
From the north a start should be made at the railway/road bridge (GR 145771). The forestry tracks are then followed to emerge at a dam (GR 162759). The Allt Daim is followed until the base of your chosen climb is reached (2½ - 3 hours).

From the south the approach begins at the head of Glen Nevis (GR 167691). Walk to Steall ruin bridge (GR 186687) and then follow the west bank of the Allt Corie Guibhsachan to the High Saddle (GR 187722). Traverse the right (east) side of the Allt Daim glen to reach the routes (2½ - 3 hours). This approach can also be used for routes on the West and North Faces of Aonach Beag. It is also a fine way to approach Carn Mor Dearg if you intend traversing the spectacular arête which links that mountain with Ben Nevis.
N.B. Care should be taken when approaching the Aonach Mor/Beag col (GR 194720) from either of the previous directions. Many accidents have occurred on this slope, especially in descent.

Aonach Mor East Face
Drive to Leanachan (GR 219786) and then follow forest rides and tracks/paths towards the Allt Cholle-rais which leads up to the base of the cliffs in Coire an Lochan (GR 198739). The 1:25,000 map is useful for this approach 3 - 3½ hours.
N.B. A rough path exists beneath the line of the Gondola which may be of use, especially in descent if the last Gondola has been missed. This is the shortest and quickest approach on foot from the valley.

Aonach Beag

An approach to the eastern facet of Aonach Beag (Stob Coire Bealach) GR 206708) and the long N.E. Ridge descending from the main summit of Aonach Beag can be made by continuing past Steal ruin to GR 215690. Then strike up the hill to the north, aiming for the col 731m (1:25,000 map, GR 211705). From here a long and tiring traverse of the corrie must be made to the foot of the N.E. Ridge, 3 - 3¹/₂ hours.

Gondola Approach

Having studied the detail and digested the time involved in the previous methods of approaching these climbs it may become clear that 'shelling out' £3.50 return (1990 prices), is a small price to pay for a day's climbing!

The uplift facilities can be found by turning right (GR 143771) after driving three miles north out of Fort William. It is worth phoning before you leave to find out if the Gondola is running, as it is frequently affected by the strong winds blowing in this area, Tel: Fort William (0397) 705825/6

The Gondola reaches 650 metres (GR 186756 approximately).

From here it is possible to traverse south-west into the Allt Daim (descend 50m through steep ground) for climbs on the West Face of Aonach Mor, 1 - 1¹/₂ hours.

Two approaches for climbs on the East Face present themselves.

(1)   Traverse east beneath Aonach an Nid then south into Coire an Lochain 1 - 1¹/₂ hours.

(2)   Ascend the ski slopes to the south aiming for the ridge (Lemming Ridge) above Aonach an Nid on your left (east). The north bounding ridge of Coire An Lochan is then used as a short steep descent, starting where it cuts into Lemming Ridge (GR 193742). Beware of large cornices in this area 1 - 1¹/₂ hours.

N.B. Due to the large cornices which can form in this area Approach (1), is recommended if parties are unsure of the cornice formations on Approach (2). Lemming Ridge is a name given by Nevis Range Ski Development. The description of Lemming *(Collins Concise Dictionary, 1988)* "A member of any group following an unthinking course towards destruction" ... You have been warned!

NORTH FACE - AONACH BEAG

AONACH BEAG SUMMIT

AONACH BEAG / MOR COL

GLEN NEVIS APPROACH

THE RAMP & BLINKERS BUTTRESS AREA

1 WHITEOUT
2 BLACKOUT
3 STAND & DELIVER (not described)
4 SELL OUT
5 ROYAL PARDON
6 KINGS RANSOM
7 MAYFLY
8 N.E. RIDGE

Aonach Beag Approaches Using the Gondola
Go over the top of Aonach Mor 2¹/₂kms (1¹/₂- 2 hours) and descend to
the Aonach Mor/Beag col previously mentioned (15 minutes). The
North Face routes and N.E. Ridge are accessible by descending to the
N.E. from this col (beware of large cornices and windslab). Routes on
the West Face are reached by descending steeply to the S.W. from the
col or approaching on foot from Glen Nevis via the old Steall ruin and
the glen of Allt Guibhsachan (2 - 2¹/₂hours).

CLIMBS ON AONACH BEAG
Aonach Beag - North Face

Mayfly   210m   Grade III*
K.Schwartz   May 1979
There is a large triangular face between the Aonach Mor/Beag col
and the N.E. Ridge of Aonach Beag. The face has a steep buttress
nearest the col, an easier gully area in the centre and a lower rocky
section. Just left of the centre (GR 197718), an initially wide gully,
marked on its lower right by a rock rib, leads to above the pinnacles
of the N.E. Ridge. This climb takes the gully. After 90m an 18m high
and equally wide icefall is reached and climbed on its right side.
Continue by a much narrower gully above which leads via an
awkward ice bulge to the easier upper section. Finish up N.E. Ridge
to the summit.

The following climbs are on the steep buttress nearest the col
mentioned in the description to Mayfly.

Whiteout   170m   Grade III
S.Richardson and R.Webb   November 1985
From the Aonach Mor/Beag col descend east and take the first
prominent icefall on the right and follow it for 50m to a snowfield.
Climb this and exit right via a short icefall to another snow slope. This
snow slope leads up to a steep buttress with a deep chimney on its
left. Climb the right side of the buttress to a final snow slope.

Blackout   120m   Grade IV/V
J.Dunn and R.G.Webb   February 1987
Climb the deep chimney passed by Whiteout in one long hard pitch
on its left wall.

Sellout   150m   Grade III
R.Webb and S.Richardson   April 1989
A left hand finish to Whiteout. Where Whiteout traverses right,
move left below a steep ice-fall (Stand and Deliver), to reach an ice
pitch to the left of a rock buttress. Climb this (30m) to reach easier
ground above.

Royal Pardon   220m   Grade V**
R.Webb and S.Richardson   February 1987
About 50m right of King's Ransom is a prominent thin ice smear
running down the centre of the buttress. Similar to Smith's Route on
Gardyloo Buttress, but with steeper and thinner ice. Climb a series of
ice falls for 55m to belay at the bottom right-hand side of the smear.
Climb the vertical smear (40m), poor belay on the right. A short pitch
up ice leads to a broad snow couloir (20m). Follow the couloir for
50m, then left up two good steep ice pitches to the summit plateau.

King's Ransom   250m   Grade V
S.Richardson and R.Webb   February 1987
The very left side of the Whiteout buttress is split by a narrow gully.
Follow the gully for two pitches until it fades. Break out right over
difficult mixed ground to the crest of the buttress. Follow easy angled
ice for 20m to the foot of a gully. Climb this steeply, passing behind
a chockstone. Continue to vertical free-standing ice pillar which is
climbed up its left-hand side (chimneying) and go left onto vertical
wall (50m). Continue up the steep gully to spike belay below
impending wall right of left edge of the buttress (40m). Follow the
ramp line on the right until it fades out (10m) and climb overhang
above (sling) to reach another ramp which is followed to crest of
buttress. A fine snow arête and mixed ground leads to the summit
plateau (90m).

N.E. Ridge   460m   Grade II/III*

J.MacLay, W.W.Naismith and G.Thomson   April 1895

The original climb on Aonach Beag, this long ridge descends well into the corrie below Aonach Beag.

From the col (GR 211705) on the Glen Nevis approach descend for 100m. Head N.N.W. for 1½- 2kms crossing three burns (second and third burns are gorge-like). Arriving at a fourth burn, the ridge is immediately above (1 hour from the col). The toe of the ridge is also approachable from the Aonach Mor/Beag col. The lower section of the ridge is not particularly difficult, but the middle part of the climb is quite narrow, with several pinnacles, which may be hard in icy conditions. Higher up the ridge becomes broader and easier, finishing about 50 metres to the north-west of the summit.

The Ramp   300m   Grade II/III

K.V.Crocket, R.Hockey, B.E.H.Maden, R.Miller and R.Pillinger   February 1975

Just north of the col (GR 211705) a prominent buttress falls towards the corrie from Stob Coire Bhealaich (GR 206708 - 1:25,000 map). Left of the crest of the buttress is a long tapering snow slope. Although it appears to be a couloir, it is in fact a ramp passing through a steep face. At the top a further 60 metres of ridge (exposed on the left) leads to the summit.

N.B. This route is best approached from Glen Nevis.

The Clare Effect   120m   Grade IV

S.Kennedy and L.Skoudas   March 1989

Above the rightward slanting ramp of the previous route, high on the left side of the buttress is a prominent right-angled corner. Enter the corner by steep ice and follow it closely to a large cornice which was tunnelled with difficulty on the first ascent.

Blinkers Buttress   300m   Grade II or IV

R.Everett, N.Barratt and S.Richardson   February 1989

The difficulties are avoidable but the climb provides a fine excursion in remote and beautiful surroundings. Start just to the right of The Ramp, below a very steep wall (50m, Grade IV but avoidable by a snow gully some way right). Snow leads to a belay beneath the steep crest of the buttress (50m). Climb a series of icy grooves to the right of the crest above (50m). Follow the ridge to the top and the upper part of The Ramp.

CLIMBS ON AONACH MOR
East Face. Coire nan Lochain

These routes come into condition quickly and early in the season due to their altitude. It should be possible to climb a number of routes in a day, as they are short and access is fairly easy. Later in the winter or after heavy snowfalls the routes will bank out and huge cornices form over some of the climbs and access routes. The climbs are described from right to left as the climber faces the corrie.

Jet Stream   100m   Grade IV**
R.Everett and S.Richardson   3rd December 1988
This is the narrow gully immediately left of the steep northerly buttress (which forms an icicle icefall in its lower part) about 50m left of the northerly bounding ridge. Climb the gully over several steep sections to a snow bay (45m). Exit right up a steep awkward wall to easier ground which leads to below the cornice (45m). Up to the cornice and over the top. Excellent climbing. When fully formed, the icefall which forms in the headwall would make an exciting and fitting direct finish.

Force Ten Buttress   140m   Grade III
R.Everett and S.Richardson   3rd December 1988
This climb takes the buttress just left of the twin icy chimneys 20m left of Jet Stream. Climb mixed ground just left of the crest then move right to a belay at the foot of a short chimney where the buttress steepens (45m). Climb the chimney then step right to climb a short difficult crack. Now climb mixed ground, mainly just to the right of the crest, to join a gully which rises to a col where the buttress merges into the final slopes (40m). The climb is technically hard for the grade, with several short, difficult, well protected sections, but the rock is very friendly!

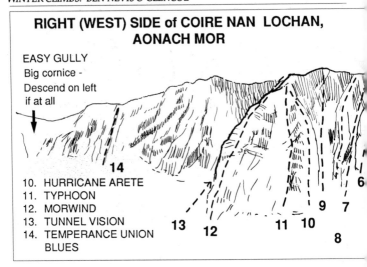

RIGHT (WEST) SIDE of COIRE NAN LOCHAN, AONACH MOR

EASY GULLY
Big cornice -
Descend on left
if at all

10. HURRICANE ARETE
11. TYPHOON
12. MORWIND
13. TUNNEL VISION
14. TEMPERANCE UNION
    BLUES

Icicle Gully   130m   Grade III
R.Everett and S.Richardson   26th November 1988
The gully to the left of Force Ten Buttress. Climb the gully line with interest to a belay on the right (50m). Take the wider line to the right of a narrow groove (which is bounded by Grooved Arête to the left). Climb this until it narrows and steepens at an icicle, which leads to a snow bay (50m). Continue up the mixed ground above (30m).

Grooved Arête   130m   Grade IV**
S.Richardson and R.Everett   26th November 1988
This superb climb takes the narrow arête immediately left of Icicle Gully. Start at the foot of the gully, gain the arête to the left and follow this, easily at first, then with increasing interest up grooves on its left side before moving back right to belay below a steep tower (45m). Climb a series of steep grooves on the crest of the tower until it is possible to move left to a ledge. Climb the short vertical corner above with difficulty, exiting on the right (35m). Regain the crest and continue more easily to the plateau (50m). Excellent technical climbing.

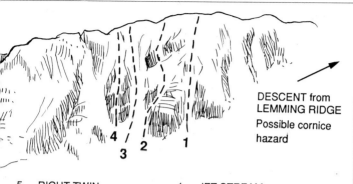

5.	RIGHT TWIN	1.	JET STREAM
6.	SIAMESE BUTTRESS	2.	FORCE 10 BUTTRESS
7.	FORGOTTEN TWIN	3.	ICICLE GULLY
8.	THE SPLIT	4.	GROOVED ARETE
9.	LEFT TWIN		

Right Twin   120m   Grade II
S.Richardson and R.Everett   22nd January 1989
There is a further 100m of cliff left of Grooved Arête before the deep cut gully of Right Twin. About 1½ metres wide with vertical side walls, it gives an enjoyable traditional climb with steep sections at the bottom and at mid-height. Exit left at the top.

Siamese Buttress   120m   Grade II*
S.Richardson and R.Everett   19th February 1989
The well defined buttress left of Right Twin provides an enjoyable scramble. Harder (Grade III) if started up the steep corners on the left.

Forgotten Twin   120m   Grade I/II
R.Everett and S.Richardson   22nd January 1989
A short leftward ramp from the foot of Right Twin leads to an easy gully with a couple of steeper stretches before the cornice exit. If the cornices are impassable it should be possible to reach and descend this climb from all the routes in the central area.

The Split 130m Grade III
S.Richardson and R.Everett 19th January 1989
The left-hand side of the buttress left of Forgotten Twin is split by a deep chimney. Start at the foot of the buttress and climb the introductory chimney to snow slopes to the right of Left Twin (25m). Enter the deep chimney and continue under several large jammed blocks until it is possible to exit to the left some 4m below the final overhang. Continue up the arête to belay (45m). Climb easy snow leftwards to join Left Twin (50m).

Left Twin 120m Grade III**
R.Everett and S.Richardson 22nd January 1989
The obvious gully a few metres left of Forgotten Twin and immediately right of Central Buttress. It is climbed direct and is comparable in quality and difficulty to SC Gully. Belays and runners hard to find.

Hurricane Arête 140m Grade V
S.Richardson and R.Everett 4th March 1989
The slabby Central Buttress, left of Left Twin, is the highest section of crag in the coire. On its right-hand side is a steep arête, with several overhangs in its upper section, which forms the left wall of Left Twin. This hard climb takes an intricate line through the overhangs just left of the arête. Start mid-way between Typhoon and Left Twin.

Typhoon 130m Grade IV*
R.Everett and S.Richardson 14th January 1989
This excellent climb takes a direct line up the grooves just left of Hurricane Arête. Climb the lower slabby grooves to a belay at the base of a chimney (40m). Climb the chimney and the groove past an overhang (30m). Continue direct on steep ice to exit on to the final slopes (40m).

Morwind 150m Grade III**
R.Everett and S.Richardson 10th January 1988
Takes a direct line up a series of grooves on the crest of Central Buttress, starting from the lowest rocks about 30m left of Typhoon. A good technically interesting climb. Climb a short gully leading to a shallow chimney line with several tricky steps on the crest. This

leads to a small bay beneath a cave after two pitches. Exit right up mixed ground to easier slopes beneath the cornice (which could be very large late in the season).

Tunnel Vision   120m   Grade III
S.Richardson and R.Everett   22nd January 1989
Start at the foot of the gully immediately left of Morwind. An initial narrows leads to a snow bay with three possible exits. Climb ice smears up the wall at the back of the bay with interest, in an exposed position, to a steep cornice exit. In full conditions the wall may bank up to a frightening angle and the cornice becomes impassible. The left branch would provide a steep and technical alternative and it should always be possible to climb the right branch to reach the easy upper section of Morwind.

Temperance Union Blues   90m   Grade III
S.Richardson, G.Armstrong, C.Millar and J.Owens   18th February 1989
50m to the right of the large open descent gully (some 200m left of Morwind) is a deep cleft at half-height. Climb either of two converging lines to the bottom of the cleft (45m). Ascend the cleft, exiting where it steepens on to a ramp which is followed to the cornice (45m).

Hidden Gully   120m   Grade II*
R.Webb and C.Rice   21st January 1989
At the south end of the coire, some way left of the open descent gully is an attractive narrow twisting couloir.
N.B. Some of these routes may well have been climbed by RAF Mountain Rescue Team members in the fifties and sixties, but never recorded.

CLIMBS ON THE WEST FACE OF AONACH MOR
The West Face of Aonach Mor presents several granite ridges of moderate angle but over 300m high. The steepest of these are directly below the summit cairn, and being in a slightly recessed bay, they are hidden from many viewpoints. The climbs provide excellent mountaineering routes on superb rock in a wild and remote setting.

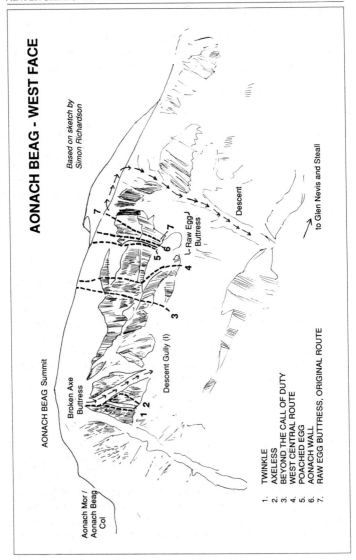

AONACH BEAG - WEST FACE

Based on sketch by
Simon Richardson

AONACH BEAG Summit

Broken Axe
Buttress

Aonach Mor /
Aonach Beag
Col

Descent Gully (I)

Raw Egg
Buttress

Descent

to Glen Nevis and Steall

1. TWINKLE
2. AXELESS
3. BEYOND THE CALL OF DUTY
4. WEST CENTRAL ROUTE
5. POACHED EGG
6. AONACH WALL
7. RAW EGG BUTTRESS, ORIGINAL ROUTE

Western Rib 300m Grade II/III
S.Richardson 17th December 1988
From below, the second buttress from the left appears as a flying buttress joining the third, broader buttress (Daim Buttress). A delightful long route with sustained interest, never very hard.

Daim Buttress 300m Grade II/III
R.Everett, N Barratt and S.Richardson 25th February 1989
This is the third buttress from the left, characterised by a prominent slab just above half-height. Start directly below the slab at the foot of the buttress. The first 200m gives enjoyable mixed climbing up snow and rocky corners to ledges at the foot of the slab. Move left and climb cracks on the left edge of the slab to a platform (50m). Take the cracks and corners up the buttress above (50m). Scrambling leads to the top in 200m.

Many more variations are possible in this area.

CLIMBS ON AONACH BEAG WEST FACE
In clear weather the main features of this face are easily seen from the top of N.E. Buttress or the Abseil Posts and climbers in that area could help themselves by spying out the lines when on Ben Nevis. Moving south from the Aonach Beag/Mor col the first feature is a broad gully bounded on its right by Broken Axe Buttress which has another deep easy gully on its right. Right of this gully is a lot of broken ground which form several icefalls before arriving at the most prominent buttress, Raw Egg Buttress (approx. GR 191711) some 700m south-west of the col. The climbs are described as if approaching from the col.

Twinkle 150m Grade IV
R.Everett and S.Richardson 20th February 1988
An excellent mixed route which follows the crest of Broken Axe Buttress directly. Technically quite hard for the grade, but well protected and with several escapes possible to easier ground. Climb a chimney-groove to the left of the steep wall left of Axeless, then move right to belay above the wall (30m). Climb the open groove above to a small ledge, step right and climb the continuation groove

to a small col junction with Axeless (40m). Step right to a steep corner. Climb this and the overhanging chimney above then continue direct to join the final easy arête (50m). Follow Axeless to the top.

Axeless 150m Grade III
R.Webb and R.Everett 16th January 1988

This climb takes an indirect but interesting line up Broken Axe Buttress. Start at a steep wall at the foot of the buttress in a small snow bay. Climb a groove on the right to a ledge overlooking the gully. Step right on to steep ice and climb up to snow which leads back left to the crest of the buttress at a col. Move left to avoid the steep step above, then trend back right to gain a fine ridge which leads to the top.

Beyond the Call of Duty 150m Grade III
R.Everett and S.Richardson 20th February 1988

This climb takes the prominent series of icefalls which form in the centre of the face between Raw Egg and Broken Axe buttresses. The first is easy angled, the second is a standing pillar approached from the right and the third starts steeply but eases higher up. Snow slopes then lead to the top.

West Central Route 150m Grade II
R.Everett and R.Webb 16th January 1988

A fine open mountaineering line to the right of Beyond the Call. Follow open grooves to belay at the right end of the rock wall which is to the right of the second pitch of Beyond the Call. Climb the icefall to the right, then follow snow to a right-facing groove high on the face. Follow this then snow to the top.

Poached Egg 120m Grade III
R.G.Webb and J.Dunn 21st February 1987

The groove system left of Raw Egg Buttress.

Eggsclamation 150m Grade II
S.Richardson and R.Everett 5th April 1987

Immediately left of Raw Egg Buttress is an icy couloir. Follow this over short steps until the main line trends left (Poached Egg). Climb a short wall to gain the steeper direct continuation which finishes next to the final rocks of the buttress.

Aonach Wall   150m   Grade V
R.Everett and S.Richardson   27th March 1988
This climb takes a direct line just to the right of the left arête of Raw
Egg Buttress, taking in enjoyable technical climbing of steadily
increasing difficulty. Start to the left of Raw Egg Buttress below the
steep tower with the prominent perched block. Climb up and avoid
the tower on the right to belay by the notch - as for Raw Egg Buttress
(55m). Climb directly up via a short corner to gain snow below a
longer corner which leads to the crest of the arête (40m). Easy snow
leads to the base of the headwall (20m). Climb a groove and wide
crack straight above to a ledge (20m). Move right to gain the obvious
V-groove which provides the only line up the final wall. Climb this
with difficulty to the top (15m).

Raw Egg Buttress   180m   Grade IV
R.Everett and S.Richardson   5th April 1987
A good, well-protected mixed climb with several short difficult steps
which takes a line up the front face trending from left to right. Start
to the left of the lowest rocks on the left side of the crag. Climb an icy
groove to below an overhanging corner, and then traverse right
below a steep wall until it is possible to climb it (30m). Now trend up
and left over mixed ground to belay next to a notch in the ridge on the
left, formed by a tower with a prominent perched block (50m).
Follow the icy groove line above for two long pitches, always
trending right, over several steep steps and corners (85m). The last
pitch takes a steep corner to the left of a steep wall and has a difficult
exit (15m).

Heading towards the very narrow pinnacled section on the Aonach Eagach between Meall Dearg and Stob Coire Leith.

GLENCOE

GLENCOE (See map on back endpaper)

The peaks of Glencoe are all considerably lower than those of Ben Nevis and the Aonachs and good conditions are therefore less certain. Nonetheless, this area provides a wider range of route choice, especially in the lower grades, than does The Ben. The ridges which abruptly separates the deep glens and corries are all fine outings, whilst the ridge and corrie walls provide excellent winter climbing to all standards. Indeed it could be argued that the 'Coe' is at the leading edge of modern winter climbing on Scotland's west coast.

Recent developments of the techniques of torqueing (jamming and twisting both axe and hammer into steep, rocky, snow-covered natural crack lines, in order to make progress) have pushed standards of difficulty upwards in Glencoe. Albeit away from the traditional snow/ice climb. Generally the ice climbing in Glencoe when in condition will be of the frozen waterfall/drainage weeps variety, unlike Ben Nevis which provides more frozen atmospheric rime ice cover due to its higher elevation.

Another major advantage over Ben Nevis are the shorter approaches, especially when starting from higher up the glen. Some routes on 'The Buachaille' for example can be started after only an hour's walk. Descent routes from all of the peaks should be treated with extreme care due to the steep and rocky nature of this area.

CLIMBS ON THE WEST FACE OF AONACH DUBH

The west face of Aonach Dubh which faces Clachaig Inn is a vast and complex series of buttress and gullies. If the snow level is low the face comes quickly into condition and so provides one of the more popular cliffs in the Glen. The buttresses are split horizontally into three tiers by Middle Ledge (between the lowest and middle tiers) and The Rake (between middle and upper tiers). Splitting the face vertically are six main gullies numbered from left to right and there are two scoops which split the main mass of the middle tier. The best

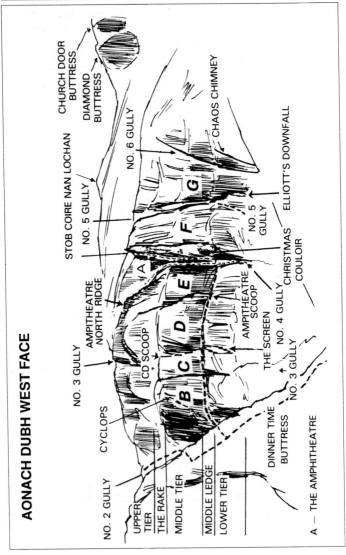

AONACH DUBH WEST FACE

CHURCH DOOR BUTTRESS
DIAMOND BUTTRESS
NO. 6 GULLY
CHAOS CHIMNEY
STOB COIRE NAN LOCHAN
NO. 5 GULLY
ELLIOTT'S DOWNFALL
NO. 3 GULLY
AMPITHEATRE NORTH RIDGE
NO. 5 GULLY
A
F
G
E
D
C
B
CD SCOOP
CYCLOPS
AMPITHEATRE SCOOP
THE SCREEN
NO. 4 GULLY
CHRISTMAS COULOIR
NO. 2 GULLY
UPPER TIER
THE RAKE
MIDDLE TIER
MIDDLE LEDGE
LOWER TIER
NO. 3 GULLY
DINNER TIME BUTTRESS

A — THE AMPHITHEATRE

approach is from the bridge (GR 137566) on the main road at Clachaig road end and up to the right of the stream until above the waterfalls. Cross the stream and gain access to the climbs. The safest descent is to go over the bridge and down into Coire nan Lochan or right into Coire nam Beith but the quickest way, in good visibility, is by the easy upper part of No.2 Gully and the lower part of Dinner-time Buttress.

Dinner time Buttress   335m   Grade I/II*

Lies on the left-hand side of the face below the col between the Nose of Aonach Dubh and Stob Coire nan Lochan. It is defined by the vague No.1 Gully on the left and by the deep watercourse of No.2 Gully on the right. Except for the final section it is mainly grass with short sections of scrambling. Can be used to approach the climbs on Stob Coire nan Lochan. A good bad weather route.

Various options can be found on reaching the final rocky section, and all are worthwhile.

(1)   Traverse left into No.1 Gully. Grade I/II.
(2)   Climb a short awkward chimney in the frontal face of the buttress between No.1 and 2 gullies, followed by some interesting scrambling Grade II.
(3)   Traverse right into No.2 Gully. Grade 1.
(4)   Climb an icy gully up left at the point where No.2 Gully is entered Grade II.

Middle Ledge Rake   Grade II

Gained from No.2 Gully, the ledge gives an exposed if easy traverse. The only difficulty lies in the initial pitch out of No.2 Gully. On reaching No.4 Gully ascend the middle section of the gully without difficulty and escape left along the Rake. Impressive scenery.

Cyclops   105m   Grade III/IV
H.MacInnes and party   January 1970

At the start of Middle Ledge a steep corner goes directly up B Buttress. Climb this to easier ground. Take the chimney line above to gain an eye in the buttress. From the other side of the eye climb iced rocks to the top.

No.3 Gully   300m   Grade II/III*
Crofton and Evans   March 1934
This gully immediately right of B Buttress is shallow and rather indefinite except where it cuts through the middle tier. Often gives a good ice pitch at the start. The top part, often avoided by The Rake, is well worth doing.

The Screen   75m   Grade IV**
D.Bathgate and J.Brumfitt   February 1965
The obvious large icefall which forms over the lowest tier of rocks to the right of No.3 Gully. Climb for 25m to an icicle recess (good runner), step left and move up to rock belays on the left. Trend right to Middle Ledge. An enjoyable and popular route.

The Smear   75m   Grade III/IV*
I.Clough and party
This icefall lies on the right wall of No.3 Gully where it cuts the middle tier. A pleasant climb which can provide a suitable continuation to The Screen.

The Flute   75m   Grade IV
D.Cuthbertson and E.Todd   1979
Just to the right of The Screen is a narrow icy chimney which gives the line of the climb.

C Buttress   150m   Grade II
J.McArtney, A.Smith, A.Thompson, A.Taylor and K.Withall   February 1969
Enter by the lower part of B Buttress and Middle Ledge and climb the middle tier by a short, wide chimney. Continue up the well defined crest.

C-D Scoop   150m   Grade II
D.Bathgate and J.Brumfitt   February 1965
The easy gully splitting the middle tier above The Screen.

D Buttress   150m   Grade II/III
I.Clough, J.Choat, J.Friend, P.Mallinson and D.Power   February 1969
Climb a steep icy gangway just to the right of C-D Scoop from the

Middle Ledge. Above, zig-zag ramps and ledges lead to the crest where a steep grooved wall leads to easier ground.

Amphitheatre Scoop Direct   240m   Grade IV/V***
I.S.Clough, G.Lowe and J.Hardie   February 1966
To the right of the middle tier of D Buttress is a well defined gully with a steep ice pitch above Middle Ledge. Start beneath the lower tier directly below this gully. Climb the lower tier by a steep ice chimney (crux) and continue by the ice pitch to gain the easy upper gully. One of the best climbs on the face.

Amphitheatre North Ridge   100m   Grade II
I.Clough and party   27th January 1969
Starts above and slightly right of the easy upper gully of Amphitheatre Scoop and goes up a series of cracks and grooves in the fine crest.

No.4 Gully   300m   Grade III/IV
J.Brown and D.Whillans   December 1952
The obvious deep gully near the centre of the face has several pitches in the lower part but unfortunately rarely has its deep-cleft finish in true condition. Gives an interesting route when combined with Christmas Couloir.

Christmas Couloir   240m   Grade III/IV*
I.Clough and D.G.Roberts   25th December 1965
From the easy middle section of No.4 Gully move up and right to the foot of the icefall which drops from an obvious couloir to the right of No.4 Gully onto The Rake. Climb the icefall by a long pitch and continue more easily to a choice of three steep finishes.

No.5 Gully   300m   Grade III*
A.Fyffe, C.MacInnes and N.Clough   18th February 1969
A gigantic icicle forms on the overhanging wall directly below this gully, so start to the left at the short leftward slanting gully. Climb this gully (crux) to a cave. Exit by a steep ice wall on the right and head up right to the main gully. This leads, with one steep short pitch to easy slopes.

Elliot's Downfall   115m   Grade V**
D.Cuthbertson   February 1979
The gigantic icicle (prone to collapse) below No.5 Gully gives an extremely steep and serious lead. Two easier pitches then lead to No.5 Gully.

No.6 Gully   240m   Grade III/IV***
D.Munro and P.Smith   30th March 1951
The long gully on the right side of the face usually gives about four good pitches, the last one being the crux. A popular climb, recommended.

Chaos Chimney   135m   Grade II/III*
A.Fyffe, E.Viveash, B.Jenkins, P.Hardman and J.Snodgrass   February 1969
The chimney gully going slightly right from the foot of No.6 Gully can be difficult in a poor build-up. Generally it offers three short sections.

Squaddie's Climb   130m   Grade II/III
P.Moores and party   February 1980
An ice-flow often forms on the ground to the right of Chaos Chimney giving unserious practice in front pointing.

CLIMBS ON THE NORTH FACE OF AONACH DUBH

The face is dominated by the huge dark recess of Ossian's Cave. The cave itself is situated above a terrace, Sloping Shelf, which slants up from left to right and starts at the apex of the approach triangle. The right leg of this approach triangle is formed by a gully containing many waterfalls and lying to the left of the vegetatious terrace walls which rise from the floor of the glen to Ossian's Cave. The left leg is a slanting grassy ramp topped by cliffs which are split by a huge Y-shaped gully, Findlay's Gulch. The main climbs lie on either side of Findlay's Gulch but to the left of Ossian's Cave. The path up the right side of the triangle is often icy, so the recommended approach is along the grassy ramp (as the climbs are described) after crossing the River Coe as for the direct walk into Stob Coire nan Lochan.

AONACH DUBH NORTH FACE

Diagram by Ed. Grindley

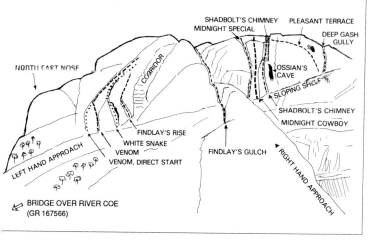

To the left of Findlay's Gully is a broad corridor which slants up right into the top of the gully. The icefall of Findlay's Rise starts at the foot of this corridor and rises on the left wall.

The steep and grassy nature of the approaches to all of the climbs provide a potentially dangerous base for avalanches after heavy snow falls or during thaw conditions.

Venom   240m   Grade IV/V**

A.McAllister, M.Duff, R.Anderson and D.Brown   January 1979

Start about 30m left of Findlay's Rise below a steep chimney in the initial buttress. Climb the long chimney to trees and move left to gain and climb the gully left of White Snake. To the left of the initial pitch is a less obvious chimney which can be taken as a direct start to the main gully.

White Snake   240m   Grade IV**

R.Anderson, A.McAllister, D.Brown and M.Duff   January 1979

Climb the icefall just to the left of Findlay's Rise to a cave formed by a huge block. Follow a left slanting ramp then more easily up a gully to a roof. Traverse left to avoid the roof, regain the gully and continue to the top.

Findlay's Rise   240m   Grade IV**
I.Nicholson and party   1978
Start at the icefall at the foot of the left wall of the corridor. A fine water-ice climb. Move steeply left onto the foot of the ice and climb less steeply to a small cave and belay. A long pitch leads to the top of the icefall from where mixed ground gives access to the summit.

Findlay's Gulch   240m   Grade III*
H.MacInnes and C.Williamson   February 1979
Above and slightly to the left of the apex of the approach triangle is a huge Y-gully. An unusual route, not as hard as it looks. Climb above the path to gain the gully at 15m. Easy ground leads to an ice wall going left to a cave. The upper section of the gully is gained by a through route leading to an easy exit.

Midnight Special   300m   Grade IV*
I.Clough and K.Spence   1969
The prominent depression to the left of Ossian's Cave starting just up to the right from the apex of the approach triangle. From the bottom of the depression climb a steep pitch (crux) to reach a shallow gully. Climb this and bear left to reach the summit slopes or finish directly by the line of the depression.

Midnight Cowboy   370m   Grade V
D.Knowles, Dud Knowles and W.Thomson   1974
Follows the line of an obvious gully running straight up, left of Shadbolt's Chimney. Start midway between Shadbolt's Chimney and Midnight Special. Follow iced walls and a chimney into the deepening gully which is followed with difficulty and poor protection to the top.

Shadbolt's Chimney   300m   Grade IV
D. and R.Goldie   13th February 1955
A deep chimney goes up from Sloping Shelf to the right of Midnight

Cowboy start and not far below and to the left of Ossian's Cave. This gives the first 45m of the climb. The route then uses the grassy buttress on the right to avoid loose section before a difficult 10m chimney leads on to an amphitheatre on the direct finish of Midnight Special. Finish up this. Rarely in condition.

Fingal's Chimney   190m   Grade V/VI
W Tauber and D.Gardner   1969

A fine sustained mixed climb requiring a lot of snow to be in good condition. One of the longest chimney climbs in the area. Only two known ascents to date.

Right of Ossian's Cave are two narrow chimneys cutting the big wall. Climb the right-hand one. From the base of the chimney a series of ledges run down rightwards, terminating by a pinnacle. Start at the pinnacle and climb its right edge. A delicate traverse left beneath overhangs is made to a ramp which leads to the base of the chimney (45m). Climb the chimney in three long pitches to Pleasant Terrace. Either continue easily up the chimney or traverse left into Shadbolt's Chimney which can be followed to the top.

Pleasant Terrace   270m   Grade III*
J.McArtney, I.Clough and party   4th January 1969

This climb and Deep-Gash Gully both start from the upper right-hand end of Sloping Shelf. The Shelf itself may give difficulty in icy conditions and the best route may be to cross the gully to gain the ridge on the right. Deep-Gash Gully is obvious - immediately above the end of The Shelf. The entry pitches to gain the start of Pleasant Terrace proper start from a bay to the left of Deep-Gash Gully and consists of two pitches. The Terrace, which soon narrows to a thin and sensational ledge leads horizontally left for a long way.

After a slight descent the ledge broadens again below a deep chimney. Climb this with difficulty to the top.

Deep-Gash Gully   65m   Grade III/IV
J.Cunningham and M.Noon   24th February 1957

This short gully at the top of Sloping Shelf can give a hard, technical problem but often banks out with snow.

CLIMBS FROM COIRE NAM BEITH

The magnificent northern corrie of Bidean is contained in the horseshoe ridges linking Stob Coire nan Lochan, Bidean nam Bian, Bidean's West Top, Stob Coire nam Beith and the nose of An-t-Sron. The main cliffs are the Diamond and Church Door Buttresses on the north face of Bidean nam Bian, the westward facing cliff on the flank of the north spur of the west top and the immense cliff cone leading to the summit of Stob Coire nam Beith.

The main approach for this corrie starts from the road junction (GR 137566) through a gate immediately west of a road bridge spanning the River Coe. The path climbs steeply to the south and after about an hour levels off into a short gorge. At this point it is better to descend to the stream bed and follow either side of the stream uphill to avoid steep slabs below the deteriorating path. One will soon arrive at a stream junction. Straight ahead the left (east) bank of the main stream can be followed towards the col between Stob Coire nam Beith and An-t-Sron. From this col a steep but straightforward approach can be made to the summit of Stob Coire nam Beith: the west and main tops of Bidean. It also provides a good method of descent from all routes starting in this corrie.

A glance at the map (Sheet 41 - 1:50,000) will reveal three streams departing from the junction previously mentioned (GR 138554). If the vague central branch is followed it leads up into Summit Gully (described later). This stream approach can provide a good reference point for parties climbing on the complicated cliffs of Stob Coire nam Beith. The left-hand stream can also be followed in a south-easterly direction through a steep band of rock bluffs into the corrie beneath the cliffs. A waterfall will be encountered on this approach and is best avoided to the right (west).

The corrie continues up to a higher basin (often referred to as the Bidean Corrie) beneath the Church Door and Diamond Buttresses. Leading up steeply on either side of these two big buttresses are easy slopes to the cols between Stob Coire nan Lochan and Bidean and between Bidean and the West Top. Both of these give descent routes but care should be exercised as they can become very icy. The right (west) of this upper basin is another subsidiary corrie which leads up between the cliffs of the West Top Spur and Stob Coire nam Beith, to a shallow col between the two summits. This gives another descent route although one should not glissade as there are a number of small rock outcrops in the corrie which may be hidden from above.

This route should be treated with care, especially if avalanche conditions prevail on north-facing slopes. In good conditions it is best to head well right in descent until an open snow slope is seen avoiding any cliffs.

AN-T-SRON (834m)   GR 134548

This mountain lies up to the right of the main approach to Coire nam Beith. On the north side of An-t-Sron is the following climb.

The Chasm of An-t-Sron   360m   Grade II/III
H.M.Brown, J.Matyssek, R.K.Graham and M.Smith   2nd January 1963
The great gully which splits the north face. The first pitch is normally turned but the other pitches higher up give good sport in icy conditions.

The following two climbs are on the east face of An-t-Sron (i.e. the right wall of the subsidiary corrie between Stob Coire nam Beith and An-t-Sron). There are several easy gullies further right towards the nose of An-t-Sron, but high in the corrie to the left of these is a big mass of crags. The right-hand section includes a big prominent smooth slab. To the left of this is a snow bay at a slightly higher level from which rise steep twin diverging couloirs. These two obvious lines give the climbs.

Sac-O-Coal Couloir   150m   Grade III
J.McArtney, D.Selby, B.Payne, J.Lines and G.Drayton   18th February 1969
The left-hand line leads to a very steep and awkward corner exit before a final easy slope leads to the summit ridge.

Smashed Spectacles Gully   150m   Grade II/III
I.Clough, F.Jones, R.Fox and C.Wood   18th February 1969
The right-hand line gives a short ice pitch in the first section and then follows a very steep chimney capped by an ice bulge before an easier continuation leads to the top.

STOB COIRE NAM BEITH (1,107m) GR 139545

The climbing on this mountain offers length, quality and variety. It will test the ability to find a route without a detailed description, especially higher up the climbs where many different options will be found. A fine peak for middle grade mountaineering routes.

The base of this massive and complicated cone of cliffs swings through a great arc so that all the climbs cannot be seen from any one viewpoint. The right-hand section is clearly seen from the junction of the stream on the approach route. The most obvious feature here is the long Summit Gully. The slabby 90m Pyramid and (above and left of it) the bigger and steeper Sphinx Buttress form an indefinite ridge which bounds Summit Gully on the left. To the left of these is the region where the vague North-West Gully winds its way through the broken rocks of No.4 Buttress. The topography of the important central section can be seen in the diagram - the unmistakable Deep-Cut Chimney, the rightward-slanting ramp gully start of No.4 Buttress, the chimney-groove line of Crack Climb and the long shallow ice course of Central Gully. Beyond Central Gully the cliffs on the left-hand side of the cone fall back and eventually form a very big bay. Arch Gully runs up the right-hand side of the bay and to the left of the lower part of this is a big rock rognon split by a narrow chimney line, the start of the so-called No.1 Buttress. Above this rognon is a broad sloping snow shelf and the continuation of the No.1 Buttress chimney-line which leads up the rocks at the back of the bay. A shallow gully curls up and round the left-hand side of the rognon to the snow shelf. This is the approach to broken Gully which has two forks, and lies in the left-hand recess of the bay. It leads up to the left to emerge on a shoulder. Beyond Broken Gully the final bold projection below the shoulder is called Zero Buttress.

The first two climbs lie on the left (east) wall of the subsidiary upper corrie between Stob Coire nam Beith and An-t-Sron. To reach these climbs follow the left bank of the stream (gorge) towards the An-t-Sron/Stob Coire nam Beith col, until above a large rock island. Hidden Gully is the obvious gully lying across to the left while Bootneck Gully is 75 metres higher up.

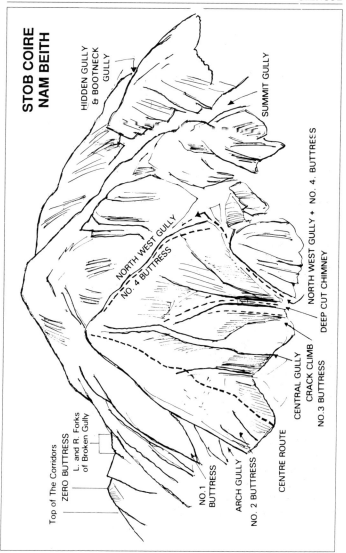

STOB COIRE NAM BEITH

HIDDEN GULLY & BOOTNECK GULLY

SUMMIT GULLY

NORTH WEST GULLY

NO. 4 BUTTRESS

NORTH WEST GULLY + NO. 4. BUTTRESS

DEEP CUT CHIMNEY

CENTRAL GULLY

CRACK CLIMB

NO.3 BUTTRESS

Top of The Corridors

ZERO BUTTRESS

L. and R. Forks of Broken Gully

NO.1 BUTTRESS

ARCH GULLY

NO. 2 BUTTRESS

CENTRE ROUTE

Bootneck Gully   245m   Grade III
H.MacInnes, I.Duckworth, P.Wells, R.Ward and J.Parsons   March 1969
Take the central chimney line for two pitches until a steep ice wall has
to be climbed. Above are easy slopes.

Hidden Gully   245m   Grade III/IV**
L.Lovat and W.Greaves   13th February 1955
Climb snow to a cave and exit to easy ground via the left wall.
Continue past another cave to a narrowing with two exits, either of
which can be taken to the ridge above.

Summit Gully   500m   Grade I/II**
The great long gully which starts just to the left of the lowest rocks of
Stob Coire nam Beith cone of cliffs. This route is often mistaken for
North-West Gully. If snow has obliterated the vague stream bed
mentioned in the earlier approach description look for the most
obvious and continuous gully line of least resistance descending
from just right (west) of the summit. This is well seen from the stream
junction of the approach route. The route is generally straightforward
with a possibility of ice steps to start with. A large cave pitch at mid-
height might be impossible but can be turned by a right-hand gully
branch 50 metres lower down. Above the cave it is straightforward
to the exit which is just right of the summit cairn.

Cleftweave   450m   Grade II/III
B.Clarke and A.Strachan   January 1972
Well to the right of North-West Gully, follow a series of gullies which
wind up left of the Pyramid to overlook Summit Gully. A steep short
ice wall on the left is followed to gullies and a snow bowl. Follow a
gully and ice pitch on the right to exit on summit slopes.

North-West Gully   500m   Grade II*
Glover and Worsdell   April 1906
Sometimes mistaken for Summit Gully to its right but distinguished
by its lack of real entry and by a ramp cutting in from the left below
No.4 Buttress. Open to considerable variation. The best start is by the
slanting ramp but steep and harder direct entries can be used. Easy
snow then leads to a fork. The left branch lacks interest so go right to

another fork amid impressive scenery. From here go to a shoulder from where a steep wall leads to easier ground.

No.4 Buttress 450m Grade II
The indefinite crest to the left of North-West Gully starting from the top of the slanting ramp.

Deep-Cut Chimney 450m Grade III/IV***
W.M.MacKenzie and W.H.Murray April 1939
The obvious deep narrow gully starting just to the left of the slanting ramp is a classic climb. The lower part gives 2 or 3 steep pitches leading at 130m to a small amphitheatre from where escape right is possible. Go up left from the amphitheatre over iced rocks to a long steep crack line which leads to easier ground. A further 200m to the summit.

Crack Climb 450m Grade III
L.S.Lovat and N.Harthill
Follows the obvious chimney-groove on the projecting side wall to the left of Deep-Cut Chimney, starting about 25m up. The line leads to the foot of a steep 10m wall which may be hard but escape to the right is possible into the amphitheatre of Deep-Cut Chimney.

Central Gully 450m Grade III/IV**
J.Clarkson and J.Waddell 12th January 1958
To the left of Crack Climb an ice-trap can form. Climb the ice-trap and follow the gully above past 3 to 4 steep pitches to easier ground. A fine climb.

Centre Route 450m Grade II/III
J.G.Parish, D.Haworth and D.McIntyre February 1945
A rather indefinite climb starting round to the left of the lowest rocks to the left of Central Gully. Zig-zag up the buttress for the initial 90m until the angle lessens.

Arch Gully 270m Grade II/III*
C.M.Allen and J.H.B.Bell December 1933
To the left of Centre Route is a shorter buttress, No.1 Buttress;

dividing the two is Arch Gully. The first section is generally banked up and leads to a couple of steep pitches which are climbed direct to a shoulder. Continue to the summit or traverse off to the left.

No.1 Buttress   270m   Grade II/III*
I.Clough and party   9th March 1967

The chimney line up the rognon left of Arch Gully and upper tier above gives a series of short ice pitches leading to the shoulder on Arch Gully.

Broken Gully   160m   Grade II
Mr & Mrs I.Clough   13th January 1966

The gully goes left up into the recess above the broad terrace which splits No.1 Buttress into two tiers. After about 30m a shallow gully on the right is followed until an easy leftwards traverse leads to the top of Zero Buttress. The left fork is a direct continuation and is separated from the normal route by a rock rib. It is steeper and holds more ice (Grade II/III).

The Corridors   160m   Grade III/IV*
I.Clough, M.A.Hudson, C.Hutchinson, C.Williamson and D.Davies
12th February 1969

To the left of Broken Gully the face of Zero Buttress is cut by two shallow square-cut gully sections; the first ending at a ledge about 45m up and the other starting from this ledge a little further to the right and leading to the top of the buttress. This gives the line of the climb. The first corridor is often only filled with powder snow so a better alternative is to take the ice ribbon leading directly up the lower slabs to the second corridor. This should then give a couple of steep pitches leading to easier ground.

THE WEST TOP OF BIDEAN NAM BIAN

Slightly higher up the corrie, these cliffs are on the western flank of the spur that descends northwards into Coire nam Beith from the West Top (i.e. the highest point of the ridge between the summits of Bidean and Stob Coire nam Beith).

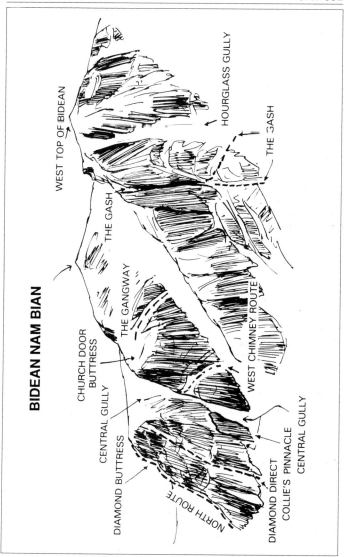

BIDEAN NAM BIAN

WEST TOP OF BIDEAN

HOURGLASS GULLY

THE GASH

THE GASH

THE GANGWAY

CHURCH DOOR BUTTRESS

CENTRAL GULLY

WEST CHIMNEY ROUTE

DIAMOND BUTTRESS

NORTH ROUTE

DIAMOND DIRECT

COLLIE'S PINNACLE

CENTRAL GULLY

The Gash   120m   Grade III/IV**
I.Clough, M.Hadley and M.Large   22nd March 1959
The steep cliffs below Hourglass Gully are split by a narrow, deep
cleft gully gained by a rising traverse leftwards from Hourglass
Gully or it may be reached directly. This gives a series of short
bulging pitches barred at the top by a chockstone. Climb this on the
left to a cave below a second huge chockstone. An intriguing through-
route should be possible.

Caradhras Cleft   125m   Grade III
T.Cuddy and L.D.Morris   March 1972
The obvious narrow gully to the right of The Gash. Start as for The
Gash and gain the gully direct or move in from Hourglass Gully.
Follow the gully to the top with a bulge where it narrows.

Hourglass Gully   120m   Grade I
The long tapering gully right of The Gash which opens into a snow
fan near the top. Steep but straightforward.

BIDEAN NAM BIAN (1,150m)   GR 143542

The summit cliffs of Bidean consist of two main buttresses divided by
a gully, Central Gully. The right-hand buttress is called Church Door
Buttress, the left-hand one Diamond Buttress.

CHURCH DOOR BUTTRESS

The Gangway   70m   Grade II
An obvious line high up on the right-hand wall of the buttress,
slanting up to the left to reach the top.

West Chimney Route   180m   Grade IV**
A.Fyffe and H.MacInnes   8th February 1969
Up to the right of the lowest rocks of the buttress is a snowy bay
leading to an obvious deep chimney, which is followed past two
difficult chockstones to a cave where there is a through-route to the
Crypt. Beyond another chimney a ledge system leads left to the top

of the Arch, an airy platform formed by two huge jammed boulders. Above a hard 10m corner chimney the route continues up left to the summit.

Crypt Route   60m   Grade IV***
H.MacInnes and party   February 1960
An unusual route wending its way through passages in the right wall of Central Gully. Climb the first pitch of Central Gully and move right to climb a steep chimney in the buttress. Where it closes step left and move through the Crypt to emerge at the Arch, a platform above the initial chimney. Finish as for West Chimney Route.

Central Gully   180m   Grade I or II** (depending on the route followed)
A fine route but with some avalanche risk. Start to the right of Collie's Pinnacle and continue directly to the top up easy slopes. By taking a start to the left of the pinnacle and using the right fork near the top, a good climb of Grade II standard will be found.

DIAMOND BUTTRESS

Direct Route   150m   Grade IV (Hard)
M.Noon and J.MacLean   January 1959
Find a way up the central wall of the buttress to gain the right end of a long ledge which cuts across the face. Continue by grooves up and to the right to emerge on the right-hand ridge shortly below the summit. A solid coating of good snow/ice is essential for this route.

North Route   210m   Grade II/III
J.Clarkson and F.King   6th February 1955
Skirts round the left end of the buttress following a series of chimneys and scoops which lead to a final rocky arête. Easy escapes are possible to the left. A slightly more difficult start (Grade III, *L.S.Lovat and W.Harrison March 1955)* is to follow an obvious steep scoop near but to the right of the normal route which leads to an arête on the right. The arête is followed by a traverse into another scoop and then the line goes up and left to join the normal route at about 80m.

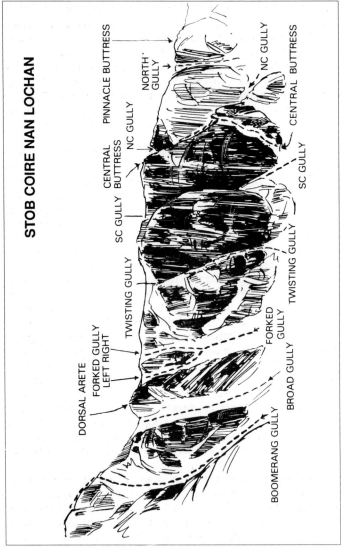

STOB COIRE NAN LOCHAN

PINNACLE BUTTRESS

NORTH GULLY

NC GULLY

NC GULLY

CENTRAL BUTTRESS

CENTRAL BUTTRESS

SC GULLY

SC GULLY

TWISTING GULLY

TWISTING GULLY

DORSAL ARETE

FORKED GULLY
LEFT RIGHT

FORKED GULLY

BROAD GULLY

BOOMERANG GULLY

CLIMBS ON STOB COIRE NAN LOCHAN (1,115m) GR 148548

This magnificent peak dominates the view between Aonach Dubh and Gearr Aonach. It is best seen to the south-west from a lay-by on the A82, (GR 168569) from where all approaches can start.

The cliffs high in the north-east facing corrie immediately below the summit of Stob Coire nan Lochan usually give good winter climbing even when lower level cliffs are spoiled by thaw. The floor of the corrie is at about 800m and the cliffs, which have an average height of 165m are arranged in a semi-circle below the summit and the shoulder extending northwards from it.

Probably the most attractive approach is by the ridge of Gearr Aonach. After crossing the bridge below the Meeting of Three Waters (GR 173561) and following the track up towards Coire Gabhail (Lost Valley) as far as the beginning of the gorge section (about a half km above the bridge) the route cuts up to the right aiming for the cliffs of the East Face of Gearr Aonach some distance to the left of the Nose.

The route up the flank to the top of the Nose is known as the Zig-Zags (grade I-II) (See diagram p135). Although marked by occasional cairns the route is not too easy to follow and it is wise to try and pick it out from well below. Careful inspection will reveal two obvious slanting terraces, up to the right and then back to the left winding up through otherwise sheer cliff. The Zig-Zags are gained by walking leftwards up a grass slope below the cliffs until the start of the first terrace is reached in a corner immediately to the right of a 15m prow of rock. After about 30m of scrambling the terrace leads gently up to the right under some steep cliffs to an easy slope which is followed for another 30m or so before taking a short slab and gully corner on the left. This leads to a second big terrace which is followed to its left-hand end. After a short ascent, another long rightward rising traverse and a brief tack back to the left leads to at the big cairn at the top of the Nose of Gearr Aonach. The ridge is then followed until an easy traverse can be made into the floor of the corrie, (about 2½ hours from the road).

This route is difficult to find in descent and, without prior knowledge and certainly in bad visibility, the valley route (next described) is preferable. Although it is not so attractive from the scenic point of view, the approach by the valley leading up between Gearr Aonach and Aonach Dubh is slightly faster than the previous route and more straightforward, and safer.

The bridge over the River Coe at GR 167566 is gained from a big lay-by on the south side of the road, east of Achtriochatan, (GR 168569). A long steady ascent up the valley eventually leads over the final lip to the floor of the corrie (2 hours).

Another possible approach is by Dinner Time Buttress on the West Face of Aonach Dubh (described elsewhere). The topography of the corrie is relatively simple. Below the summit of Stob Coire nan Lochan is Summit Buttress. This names applies particularly to the steep right-hand face, the open face and broken rocks of the left flank can be climbed anywhere at Grade I standard. To the right of Summit Buttress are Broad Gully and Forked Gully. To the right again are the South, Central, North and Pinnacle buttresses, all separated by narrow gullies.

Boomerang Gully   210m   Grade II*
J.Black, R.G.Donaldson and W.H.Murray   January 1949
This route curls round to the left of the steep rocks of Summit Buttress (and right of an indefinite rocky ridge which bounds the left flank) and swings back to finish by the ridge leading on from the top of the Buttress to the summit of the mountain. The first long tapering gully slope is followed up to the left from the foot of the steep rocks until an entry pitch on the right, rocky and frequently iced, leads up into the main couloir. If the entry pitch is missed the initial slope leads out onto the face of the left flank. The main couloir curves rightwards and leads to the final rocky arête.

Scabbard Chimney   123m   Grade IV (Hard)
L.S.Lovat, J.R.Marshall and A.H.Hendry   12th February 1956
The obvious deep chimney which starts near the lowest rocks of the steep Summit Buttress and slants up to the right. The crux is a 'sentry box' at about 65m. Above the chimney, a gully on the left leads up to the final arête. A good plating of snow and ice is essential to make this climb feasible.

Innuendo   150m   Grade IV
H.MacInnes, R.Birch, P.Judge and R.O'Shea   1969
Starts above Broad Gully, opposite and level with the foot of Dorsal Arête, below an obvious chimney-groove which leads to a ledge

cutting across the face. Climb the chimney-groove past a ledge (36m) into an overhung bay. Exit by a hard crack on the right wall and ascend more easily rightwards to a block belay below the upper wall. Traverse right beneath an overhung chimney until it is possible to climb steep cracks and gain the chimney by moving left above the overhanging section. Follow more easily up the chimney to the top.

Pearly Gates   150m   Grade II/III
I.Clough and party   17th April 1966
Leaves Broad Gully at about half-height where the side walls of Summit Buttress become more broken, and a notch is seen in the left-hand skyline. Zig-zag ramps lead up to this feature in 45m, and after passing through the 'notch' a shallow fan of snow leads directly to the summit.

Broad Gully   150m   Grade I*
A very easy route which often provides the best means of descent into the corrie but care may be required in icy conditions.

Dorsal Arête   120m   Grade II**
J.Black, T.Shepherd, J.Allingham and J.Bradburn   28th January 1951
Starting up a sprawling mass of rocks to the right of Broad Gully, the route becomes increasingly interesting as height is gained, finally tapering to a very narrow and well defined arête. Good rock belays, the climb is very useful in bad conditions.

Forked Gully Left Fork   135m   Grade I/II*
Right Fork   130m   Grade II/III*
The gully to the right of Dorsal Arête gives a steep but normally straightforward snow climb by the Left Fork. The Right Fork (right of a 60m rock rib which splits the upper section) is steeper and often iced.

Twisting Gully   150m   Grade II/III***
W.H.Murray, D.Scott and J.C.Simpson   December 1946
One of the classic Scottish snow climbs. This route takes a shallow gully immediately to the left of South Buttress and is separated from Forked Gully by an indefinite rocky rib. The first 30m lead up into a

deep recess from which there are two continuations. The normal route follows an icy chimney on the left until it bulges when a short left traverse is made across the gully wall to gain the left rib. There is an awkward mantleshelf move on the short arête which leads to easier ground. Above this crux pitch, about 30m of snow leads to another short ice pitch which can be turned on the right if necessary (this pitch may even be completely obliterated). The gully continues without difficulty to the final wide fan and a choice of steep exits.

Twisting Gully Right Fork   150m   Grade III*
J.R.Marshall and I.D.Haig   January 1958
A more difficult and more direct variation on the middle section of the normal route. From the deep recess, a very steep pitch up an ice corner is followed by a continuation runnel (separated from the original route by a broken rib) which joins the normal route below the final fan.

Moonshadow   150m   Grade III**
K.Crocket and C.Stead   January 1972
An interesting finish to the right fork of Twisting Gully. From the ice corner above the first main pitch, climb the right wall to a belay in a corner (36m). Climb this corner/groove past a chockstone to the top.

Tilt   140m   Grade V/VI***
M.Hamilton, K.Spence and A.Taylor   January 1980
A steep mixed climb with little ice and reasonable protection. To the right of Twisting Gully is South Buttress. This climb follows a very prominent chimney line just left of the blunt buttress crest. (N.B. Not to be mistaken with another prominent chimney line which starts almost at the foot of Twisting Gully and provides good climbing also, Grade V, unnamed.) Follow iced cracks to the obvious chimney and groove, (40m). Climb the groove till above an overhang. Move right with difficulty and climb a wall to belay on a large flake. Follow more grooves to a terrace and finish by a chimney and obvious V-groove on the left.

S.C. Gully   150m   Grade III***
P.D.Baird, L.Clinton and F.Clinton   March 1934
The steep gully between South and Central Buttresses is another

classic and a serious route requiring good conditions. Early in the season a steep ice pitch often bars entry to the gully but, if it is too formidable, the rib on the left may give an easier alternative. Steep snow then leads up into the bed of the gully proper. The route then traverses up to the right to gain and follow a steep ice gangway which often has a bulge shortly before the top. A long run out will normally be required to reach a satisfactory belay above the pitch. Beyond this, steep snow leads to the cornice which may be quite difficult.

Central Grooves 120m Grade VI***
K.Spence and J.McKenzie February 1983
A well protected, hard mixed route. More difficult than Tilt. To the right of S.C. Gully is Central Buttress. The climb starts at the lowest rocks and follows an obvious groove just left of the crest throughout.

Central Buttress - Ordinary Route 150m Grade III**
H.Raeburn with Dr and Mrs C. Inglis-Clark April 1907
Starts from the bay to the left of the lowest right-hand spur and goes up to the right to gain its crest. The ridge leads to a tower which is best turned on the right regaining the crest by a short chimney. A good route with splendid situations.

N.C. Gully 155m Grade I/II*
The gully between Central and North buttresses generally gives a steep but straightforward snow climb. Early in the season it may have short pitches. A good introductory gully.

Crest Route 115m Grade IV*
R.Anderson and M.Hamilton November 1985
To the right of N.C. Gully is North Buttress. This climb follows an obvious groove just right of the buttress crest and starts at the lowest rocks. It provides a good introduction to steep mixed climbing. Climb broken stepped ground, a short wall and cracks to belay on a pedestal (35m). Climb a flake crack above, and move right across a slab to gain a corner which is followed to the crest. Step left at a large spike onto a ledge (30m). Follow the groove and easy ground to the top, a short wall is overcome by a stepped flake crack on the right.

North Gully 75m Grade I/II
Divides North Buttress from Pinnacle Buttress. It is steep, sometimes gives a short pitch and often carries a heavy cornice.

Pinnacle Buttress Groove 60m Grade II/III*
H.MacInnes February 1950
Follows a steep groove on the North Gully flank of Pinnacle Buttress to the left of a prominent arête. Start on the right near the foot of North Gully. An excellent short climb in icy conditions.

Pinnacle Buttress, North-East Face 90m Grade III
L.S.Lovat and N.G.Harthill January 1958
Starts at the lowest rocks and climbs up right then left up a short groove to a steep wall. An icy corner crack on the right leads to a ledge and a higher ledge is gained up to the right. From the left end of this upper ledge an awkward chimney leads to the roof of the buttress.

To the right of Pinnacle Buttress are some short gullies and rocky outcrops which can provide good practice on a short day.

CLIMBS ON THE NORTH AND WEST FACES OF GEARR AONACH

The huge north face of Gearr Aonach dominates the ridge running between the Lost Valley and Stob Coire nan Lochan. The first two climbs described lie to the right side of this face while the remainder are situated on the steep buttress on the west face below the highest point of the ridge. All the climbs are easily reached from the path running up the east side of the stream on the approach to Stob Coire nan Lochan.

Avalanche Gully 300m Grade II/III*
H.MacInnes and party
After crossing the bridge over the River Coe the main path strikes up towards the north face of Gearr Aonach before veering up to the right. The lower stream way of this gully crosses the path at this point. In hard weather condition, the lower part gives a series of short water ice pitches. The gully follows a rightward slant and leads to the summit of the Nose. Take the right forks at the lower and upper

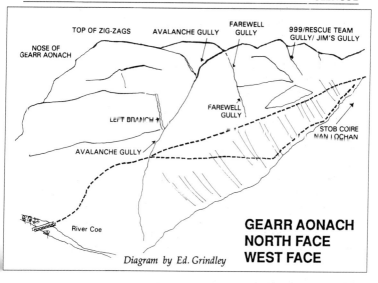

TOP OF ZIG-ZAGS   AVALANCHE GULLY

FAREWELL GULLY

999/RESCUE TEAM GULLY/ JIM'S GULLY

NOSE OF GEARR AONACH

FAREWELL GULLY

LEFT BRANCH

AVALANCHE GULLY

STOB COIRE NAN LOCHAN

River Coe

GEARR AONACH NORTH FACE WEST FACE

Diagram by Ed. Grindley

branches. The Lower Left Branch is short, steep and interesting (Grade IV).

Farewell Gully   150m   Grade II/III
J.McArtney and party   February 1969
From slightly higher up the path from Avalanche Gully, the climb goes up in a direct line to meet the finish of that route. Several short pitches, but little of interest.

The following climbs are on the buttress below the highest point of the Gearr Aonach ridge. Although short they have the attraction of easy access and rapidly come into condition after heavy snowfalls. The best approach is to follow the Stob Coire nan Lochan path till just before it steepens on entering the coire; then to strike back left into the easy entry gully. The climbs described are really three finishes to this gully.

Rescue Team Gully   85m   Grade II/III*
H.MacInnes and party   March 1966
The left-hand branch is a steep icy chimney with a through-route
chockstone at its foot. Two good pitches.

Jim's Gully   106m   Grade II/III
J.McArtney and party   March 1968
The central branch emits an icefall landing near the start of the
previous route. Above this icefall the gully is easy.

999   135m   Grade III**
H.MacInnes and party   February 1969
The right-hand branch gives a series of enjoyable short steep pitches.
Follow the most obvious line.

The following route is to the right of the 'Zig-Zags' on the North Face
of Gearr Aonach. It provides a steep and exposed mixed route when
in condition, and has the attraction of a short approach.

White Rhino   150m   Grade IV
A.Cave and M.Duff   February 1988
From the end of the first right trending rake of the 'Zig-Zags', walk
right along a ledge to small chimney and tree in an exposed position.
Climb a very obvious diagonal rake for two pitches. Go into the gully
above (steep) to a recess below overhangs. Move steeply left with
difficulty and climb ice covered slabs and grooves to easier ground
and the 'Zig-Zags' descent.
N.B. The name of this route relates to the avalanche which was seen
on the descent (top of 'Zig-Zags') after the first ascent!

CLIMBS FROM COIRE GABHAIL (Grid Square 1655)
(The Lost Valley)

Starting from lay-bys on either the north or south side of the road a
path leads down to the footbridge over the River Coe near the
Meeting of Three Waters (GR 173564). It continues up into the corrie,
first through a gorge and eventually crossing the stream and passing

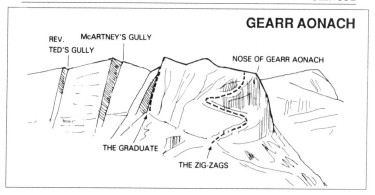

GEARR AONACH

REV. TED'S GULLY • McARTNEY'S GULLY • NOSE OF GEARR AONACH • THE GRADUATE • THE ZIG-ZAGS

through a boulder field to reach the floor of the corrie, a flat 500m of shingle and grass (45 minutes). The walk so far is very interesting and worthwhile for its own sake on an off-day. At the entrance to the corrie floor is the 10m Boulder - a useful landmark. Beyond the corrie floor there are two paths to the right of the stream and at different levels. The highest is the better of the two and makes a gradual ascent along the side of the valley until the stream is crossed above its deep gorge bed (accidents often occur here). The track disappears soon above this point and the two main approach/descent routes bifurcate. One route continues straight ahead to the col at the end of the valley - between Stob Coire Sgreamhach, 1,070m on the left and Bidean nam Bian. The slope is easy but there may be fairly large cornices. The other route bears up right into a subsidiary corrie which leads up to the col between Bidean and Stob Coire nan Lochan. Either of these are good descents but care may be required near the cornices. The cliffs of Stob Coire nan Lochan may also be reached by bearing back in a northerly direction, beyond the cliffs of the Upper East Face of Gearr Aonach, obliquely across the hillside to reach the shoulder where the Gearr Aonach ridge rises steeply towards the summit of Stob Coire nan Lochan.

LOST VALLEY ICE SLABS

On the east side of the stream emerging from the boulder field below the flat part of the Lost Valley are tiers of slabby wet rock that quickly freeze in a cold winter. Several good pitches have been made on these, steep slabs.

BEINN FHADA (GS 1654) AND STOB COIRE SGREAMHACH (GS 1553)

These two peaks link a fine ridge crest and form the steep slopes which enclose Coire Gabhail to the south-east. The ridge is steep and rocky on all sides and gained most easily from the east below point 811m (GR 172553). Ascent to this point is also possible from Coire Gabhail, starting up the steep and tedious slope two hundred metres beyond the large 10m Boulder. Take the line of least resistance and arrive at a bealach after 1 - 1½ hours of upward toil! The ridge is followed with continual interest to a rocky step (GR 157538), which should be turned on the left before ascending to the summit of Stob Coire Sgreamhach. This fine outing is similar in parts to the Aonach Eagach (Grade II). In descent the easiest route is via the bealach at GR 151537. Care should be taken on this slope. The cornice can be large and the avalanche potential considerable at certain times.

The north face of Stob Coire Sgreamhach provides long and interesting approaches to the summit at Grade II depending on the line you take. Access to this face is best by the track up the west bank of Allt Coire Gabhail as far as the stream junction beyond the gorge (GR 154543). From here, strike up the steepening slope to the south beneath the summit cone.

EAST FACE OF GEARR AONACH

These climbs are all on the right-hand side of Coire Gabhail beyond the Lost Valley Boulder. Particularly useful when conditions are poor at higher levels and for their relatively short approach. However, many of them are fine climbs in their own right and some rank with the best in Glencoe. Icy conditions are preferable. The best descent is by the Zig-zags (if the team is competent and the visibility good) on the Nose of Gearr Aonach (described under Stob Coire nan Lochan) but most people prefer to walk towards Stob Coire nan Lochan and descend into the upper part of the Lost Valley or Coire nan Lochan.

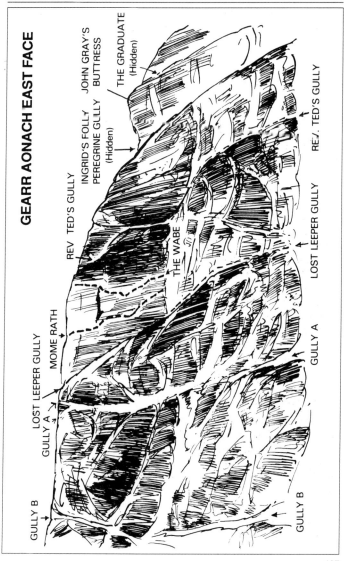

GEARR AONACH EAST FACE

GULLY B

LOST LEEPER GULLY
GULLY A

MOME RATH

REV TED'S GULLY

INGRID'S FOLLY
PEREGRINE GLLLY
(Hidden)

JOHN GRAY'S
BUTTRESS

THE GRADUATE
(Hidden)

THE WABE

REV. TED'S GULLY

LOST LEEPER GULLY

GULLY A

GULLY B

The routes are best described from right to left as one sees them in walking up the valley.

The Graduate   175m   Grade III/IV
D.A.Knowles, J.Loxham, D.Wilson and A.Wilson   8th February 1969
The boulder field which blocks the entrance to the floor of the Lost Valley is the result of a great landslide which has left a huge deep recess in the cliff of Gearr Aonach. Follow the great right-angled corner at the left-hand side of this recess it is most easily reached by going up and slightly rightwards from the Lost Valley Boulder. Rarely in condition.

Ingrid's Folly and Peregrine Gully   300m   Grade II*
G.S.W.C. party   (Glencoe School of Winter Climbing)
The foot of Ingrid's Folly is only about 5 minutes walk diagonally up the slope to the west of the Lost Valley Boulder. It is a well defined gully tucked away in a corner, much better than its appearance might suggest. The long grassy buttress to its right (and immediately left of The Graduate) is John Gray's Buttress, Grade II. Ingrid's Folly consists of several relatively easy rock pitches which give good sport when veneered in ice. Above the last pitch, where the gully gives an easy slope to the top, a 100-metre traverse to the left leads into Peregrine Gully. This gives further pitches; another cave with a through-route and an easy passage below a gigantic block which forms an archway just before the steep exit.

To the left of Ingrid's Folly and Peregrine Gully, the cliffs of Gearr Aonach give broken crags in the lower half leading to an almost continuous wide horizontal terrace. Above the terrace are a series of steep walls, unpleasantly grassy in summer but which give good winter climbing. The first big break in these upper cliffs is a large rightward facing corner - McArtney Gully.

McArtney Gully   175m   Grade II/III
H.MacInnes and G.S.W.C. party   3rd February 1969
The lower half of this big corner gully is reasonably straightforward, but the upper part is very steep. A vertical chimney is followed to a diagonal groove and corner which gives the crux.

Frostbite Wall   200m   Grade IV
H.MacInnes, A.Gilbert, P.Debbage, D.Layne-Joynt and D.Allright February 1969
Take the main line of the ice ribbon up the wall, gaining it first by a rightward traverse from the bottom of it, then back left to it some 50m up via a ledge. Climb the ice ribbon direct to the top.
N.B.   This route is usually in condition when the ice ribbon is complete from top to bottom of the cliff.

Frostbite Groove   200m   Grade IV
H.MacInnes and G.S.W.C. party   February 1969
At the point where Frostbite Wall traverses back across the obvious ledge, take the icy chimney/groove line up and slightly right. Break out left after one pitch, over ice bulge to gain ice scoop. Climb scoop and small chimney to the top.

Rev. Ted's Gully   300m   Grade II/III**
H.MacInnes and Rev. Ted   February 1960
Follows the obvious long couloir which slants leftwards up the full length of the face. The lower pitches are usually straightforward and lead to an obvious junction in the upper cliffs. Several alternatives are available. The best is to follow an ice chimney line just to the left of the ice fall at the junction, or to take the icefall direct. If the easy right branch is followed another steep chimney line will be found leading up from a bay; interesting but awkward. From the same bay an easy escape right can be made, reducing the whole climb to Grade I/II.

Given the right conditions the upper cliffs to the left of Rev. Ted's Gully give some of the most sensational ice climbing in Glencoe. The terrace below the upper wall can be reached by the lower sections of Rev. Ted's or Lost Leeper Gullies. The upper wall (Upper East or Mome Rath Face) has high up, a long barrier of overhangs. In hard conditions much of the face becomes masked with smears of ice and the overhang is decorated with a fantastic fringe of icicles which can attain 10/15m in length.

The Wabe   135m   Grade IV/V***
I.Clough, H.MacInnes and J.Hardie   16th February 1969
Approximately follows the line of a prominent icefall to the right of

the icicle fringe. A short wall is climbed. Belay on a snow ledge above the main terrace. The route then goes up slightly to the right before making a long diagonal leftward traverse across the icefall towards a prominent nose and a stance at 45m. After passing below the nose (immediately above an overhang) the route veers right then left to reach a pedestal stance below the right edge of the icicle fringe. Then move back right to climb the icefall where it passes through a recessed panel, good stance on the right above this section. The final pitch goes diagonally right and then back left. The route is sustained throughout and extremely exposed.

Jaberwock   135m   Grade V**
A.Paul and D.Cuthbertson   January 1984
Climbs the obvious icefall between The Wabe and Mome Rath Route, taking in the ice fringe at the top.

Mome Rath Route   135m   Grade IV/V***
A.Fyffe and J.McArtney   16th February 1969
The general line of the route is a long leftward slant. It starts below the icicle fringed overhang by an obvious broad ramp and continues the line up to the left into a chimney. This is followed for about 20m before going left again into another chimney which leads to a bay. A slabby ice plated rib on the left is followed by a short steep corner chimney. Again this route combines sustained technical climbing with a high degree of exposure.

Newsholme's Groove   140m   Grade V**
G.Hornby and C.Schaschke   February 1986
A broad groove between Mome Rath Route and Snowstormer, a bold line. Start at an open bay, move up right then left and climb a thin vertical step, belay. Follow the open groove above and move right along the icicle to finish up the last groove left of Mome Rath Route. Belays on ice screws may be necessary.

Snowstormer   100m   Grade V***
D.Cuthbertson, A.Paul and C.McLean   January 1984
This route follows close to the exposed edge right of Rainmaker. Climb to a belay on a pedestal above an obvious V-notch (27m).

Follow icy corners above to beneath the overlap overlooking the corner of Rainmaker, belay. Easier climbing leads to the top.

Rainmaker 100m Grade V***
D.Cuthbertson and M.Duff February 1980
At the left-hand end of the upper face, next to Lost Leeper Gully is a large ice-cased corner. Climb a long pitch up ice smears to the left of the corner and belay in a recess. Now climb the corner with a short excursion on the left wall.

Lost Leeper Gully 300m Grade III
H.MacInnes and G.S.W.C. party 13th February 1969
The shallow indefinite gully which comes down immediately to the left of the Mome Rath Face and reaches the lower slopes of the valley above the gradually rising path. The route weaves its way up through the lower crags, giving interesting route-finding, and the more distinct upper gully should give at least two good ice pitches. The belays in the main part of the gully are poor.

Gully A 235m Grade III/IV
H.MacInnes and D.Crabbe January 1964
The next gully to the left again, starting some distance beyond where the path starts rising from the floor of the Lost Valley. It runs the full height of the face, is indefinite in its lower part, deep cut in the middle and becomes a steep straightforward slope in the upper section. It faces south and is hidden until immediately below it. A pitch climbed on the left leads into the gully which is followed to the right to a bulging groove, the crux of the climb.

Gully A (Central Branch) 230m Grade IV
D.Haston and J.Stenhouse January 1969
Gully A divides at the start of the main pitch and this variation takes a line directly up a steep ice scoop.

Gully A (Left Branch) 235m Grade IV
H.MacInnes and G.S.W.C. party February 1970
This is the branch of the gully which starts as a very steep ice pitch slightly to the left of the main Gully A. Follow the gully line throughout

(escape possible halfway up on the left) and take either the chimney line above or break out right up steep iced rock.

Gully B   230m   Grade II
Probably G.S.W.C. parties
The next gully to the left of Gully A is straightforward except for one large chockstone pitch.

Gully C   230m   Grade I
Probably G.S.W.C. parties
A long shallow couloir on the extreme left before the cliffs fade out entirely. It may contain a few short pitches. Competent climbers may find this route useful as an approach to Stob Coire nan Lochan.

LOST VALLEY MINOR BUTTRESS
The smaller and left-hand of the two prominent buttresses at the head of the valley and below the middle of the ridge leading up from the col to Bidean. Routes are described from left to right.

Left-Hand Gullies   75m   Grade I
To the left of the buttress are two easy gullies separated by a rocky rib.

Left Edge Route   76m   Grade III
J.Moffat and C.Dale   February 1984
Start to the left of Chimney Route. Follow the obvious gangway up left to a short corner which is climbed to the top.

Chimney Route   75m   Grade III/IV*
R.Marshall and J.Moriarty   January 1959
The obvious deep chimney to the left of the centre of the face. A series of chockstone pitches can give considerable difficulty.

Central Scoop   85m   Grade III/IV
I.Clough and Mrs N.Clough   February 1969
This is the chimney line between Chimney Route and Right Edge. The chimney (short) starts from a platform some 13m up and the route takes this corner/chimney, then follows the buttress to the top.

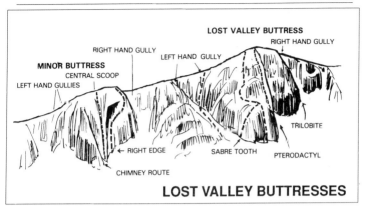

LOST VALLEY BUTTRESSES

Right Edge   120m   Grade III/IV**
J.R.Marshall, J.Stenhouse and D.Haston   February 1959
At the right-hand side of the face a broad snowfield-ramp leads up
rightwards below overhangs. Access to the ramp is gained by an icy
chimney below its left end and an arête leads from the top of the ramp
to the summit.

Right-Hand Gully   75m   Grade I
Probably G.S.W.C. parties
The gully immediately to the right of the buttress gives a
straightforward but steep climb and often has a large cornice.

LOST VALLEY BUTTRESS

The large right-hand buttress is in two distinct sections; an easier
angled left-hand portion but very steep and set back at a higher level
on the right. The routes are described from left to right.

   This cliff has been the venue for a number of hard mixed (torqueing)
routes of high quality in recent years. It should be remembered that
this type of climbing is very different from the traditional winter ice
climb which often consists of poorly protected leads on steep ice.
Torqueing (mixed) routes are often well protected with minimal
icing.

Left-Hand Gully   90m   Grade I
Probably G.S.W.C. parties
The gully is bounded on the left by a broken indefinite rib of rock.
Straightforward climbing to a steep corniced exit.

Sabre Tooth   135m   Grade III**
I.Clough and H.MacInnes   9th February 1969
There is a prominent vertical 45m corner towards the right-hand side
of the left-hand section of cliff. This has been climbed but gives a
much more difficult start which would elevate the general standard
of the climb to Grade IV/V.

Starting to the left of the corner, the route goes up into a recess and
breaks out rightwards, eventually arriving on a terrace above the big
corner. The terrace leads back left to the foot of a steep shallow 15m
corner (good belays on the left). The corner is hard for a climb of this
standard but well protected. Above it, a line of grooves is followed to
the top.

Pterodactyl (Moonlight Gully)   110m   Grade IV
H.MacInnes and D.Crabbe   January 1964
Follows the line of the shallow gully lying in the corner which divides
the two sections of cliff. The overhanging entry to the upper couloir
is difficult but relatively short. The route follows a steep corner to a
stance beneath the overhang which projects for 2 metres then climbs
to gain the upper couloir using the crack to the left of the main icicle
formation.
N.B. The central section of this route is climbed on aid and is out of
character with the rest of the route. In years of good icing it may be
possible to climb steep ice on the right of the central section.
Chockstones have recently fallen out of this section.

Neanderthal   125m   Grade VI
R.Anderson and G.Nicholl   February 1987
An improbable-looking line up the huge corner, 30 metres right of
Pterodactyl. Very good climbing according to those who have done
it! A steep mixed climb.

Easily up gully and left wall to a platform (18m). Traverse right and
climb chute to belay at a cul-de-sac (15m). Traverse right until

possible to climb to the base of corner and a small ledge (21m). Follow corner to right side of a square roof. Move left underneath this and follow recessed wall above, towards an obvious narrow slot on the skyline (27m belay). Easier climbing soon leads to the top.

Barracuda 80m Grade V (Harder on the central section)
R.Anderson and R.Milne January 1988
Another steep and difficult mixed climb. Up the obvious steep crack line which springs from the left trending ramp line right of Neanderthal. Start at the edge of the buttress. Follow the ramp to a belay at the foot of the crack. Climb the crack (with very hard initial moves) to the buttress crest. Climb the gully above to the top.

Trilobite 60m Grade II/III
H.MacInnes and I.Clough 9th February 1969
On the side wall of the buttress, leaving the right-hand gully where it begins to narrow and opposite a ramp which goes up steeply out to the right, Trilobite follows a very steep groove which runs directly up the gully wall to the top of the buttress.

Right-Hand Gully 90m Grade I/II
Probably G.S.W.C. party
A steep gully with a big cornice, often containing a small ice pitch. About 30m up, below the steepening and narrowing to the pitch and level with the runnel of Trilobite, is a variation sloping steeply up to the right - The Ramp (Grade I/II).

CLIMBS ON STOB DEARG, (GR 223543)
BUACHAILLE ETIVE MOR (1,022m)

Buachaille Etive Mor is a long ridge with four tops. Stob Dearg is the north top, a beautifully symmetrical cone as seen from the junction of the roads leading down into the glens of Etive and Coe. Of the four tops it is the highest and the only one which gives much climbing and it is generally referred to as The Buachaille.

The mountain is an excellent summer rock climbing area, whilst in winter its natural ridge and gully lines are amongst the best in Scotland. The view from the area surrounding Curved Ridge is one

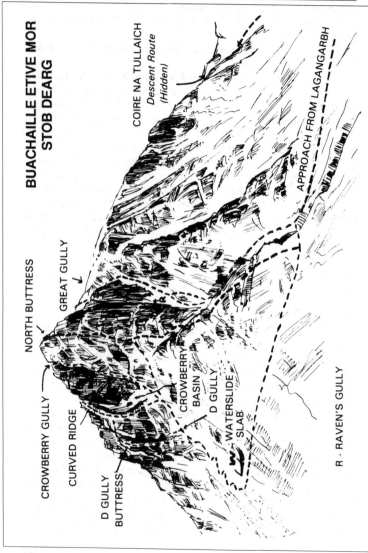

BUACHAILLE ETIVE MOR
STOB DEARG

COIRE NA TULLAICH
Descent Route
(Hidden)

APPROACH FROM LAGANGARBH

NORTH BUTTRESS

GREAT GULLY

CROWBERRY GULLY

CURVED RIDGE

D GULLY BUTTRESS

CROWBERRY BASIN

D GULLY

WATERSLIDE SLAB

R - RAVEN'S GULLY

of the most striking panoramas of any British hill.

The better routes are all on the central section of the mountain - see diagram for details.

Most of the climbs start from the Crowberry Basin - below Crowberry Ridge and Gully.

The most usual starting point is from Altnafeadh (GR 222563) on the main road (parking available in several neighbouring lay-bys). The River Coupall is crossed by a bridge leading to Lagangarbh. Beyond the hut, a track leads south-eastwards, gradually rising, to cross the foot of Great Gully after about 1¼kms. From this point one can take a shortcut by following the lower easy part of North Buttress and bearing left into the basin below Crowberry Ridge. Alternatively one can continue following the track below North Buttress, which rises slowly to meet the prominent waterslide slab. From this slab ascend straight up the steep and loose, heather and scree slopes to its left. Higher up a delicate traverse right must be made above steep rocky ground in order to gain the foot of Crowberry Gully or Curved Ridge (1½ hours).

For climbers new to this area it is advisable to drive along the main road towards the Kingshouse in order to view the main features of the mountain before choosing a route.

Descent

There is only one reasonable descent route in winter. From the summit follow the fairly level ridge for 300 metres (250° Grid). Then change course to 270° (Grid) and descend to reach a shallow cairned col at the head of Coire na Tulaich (more usually called Lagangarbh Corrie). This section can be particularly difficult in white out conditions. There are occasional cairns but it may be necessary to stay roped up and take both front and back bearings to keep on course. The most common mistake is to continue too far south-west and descend into Glen Etive. This slope is not too difficult but it is a long walk back on the road. Care should be taken not to stray too far to the north too early as there are some large crags at the head of Coire na Tulaich. From the col a steep initial slope leads down into the corrie. This slope is often in a hard icy condition and it may be best to wear crampons and to belay. Even in soft conditions it is better not to glissade as there are often boulders and screes exposed lower down.

There have been many accidents here. The lower part of the corrie (there is a track down the left-hand side) leads easily down to Lagangarbh and the road.

Also it is possible to ascend slightly from the col to point 903m (GR 214542) and descend north by the ridge to the west of Coire na Tulaich. All the large outcrops on this descent are avoidable by moving left and the ground is more interesting than Coire na Tulaich. The routes are described as they are approached from Lagangarbh.

Great Gully   360m   Grade I/II*
Norman Collie   1894

This is the first deep gully to cross the path about 20 minutes from Lagangarbh. It is sometimes confused with easier gullies further west. Early in the season it can give several hundred feet of ice, but generally banks out with frequent and considerable avalanche danger.

Raven's Gully   135m   Grade V**
H.MacInnes and C.Bonington   14th February 1953

The dark slit high up on the North Buttress (left) wall of Great Gully. When in condition (fairly often) the crux is soon reached, a large chockstone. Above three or four long difficult pitches lead to the top. A popular classic. The Direct Finish is rarely in condition.

A descent into Great Gully can be made after finishing Raven's Gully. This is only advised if avalanche potential is low and daylight is available to find a route down.

Cuneiform Corner   60m   Grade IV
A.Paul and D.Sanderson   17th March 1979

To the right of Raven's Gully is a large buttress (Cuneiform Buttress) which overlooks Great Gully. Mid-way up this buttress an obvious icefall/corner is followed in two pitches to a terrace from where a traverse right into Great Gully can be made.

N.B. It is possible to continue to the summit by following steep corners/grooves and icy walls above the traverse line for another 170m (P.Moores and C.Butler February 1983 Grade III).

Slime Wall is the very steep rocky cliff left of Raven's Gully and overlooking Great Gully.

Guerdon Grooves   180m   Grade VI+
D.Cuthbertson and A.Paul   28th January 1984
Technical and very serious with poorly protected leads on steep rock
and ice. The belays are satisfactory! The obvious icy grooves to the
left of Raven's Gully are followed for three pitches into Raven's Gully.
From the flake belay in Raven's Gully the left-hand finish is taken.

Misty High   195m   Grade IV**
A.Paul and D.Sanderson   17th March 1979
This climb follows an icefall on the extreme left side of Slime Wall. Up
the icefall and follow the right-hand chimney. Climb easier ground
to a short chimney and under a chockstone to North Buttress. Follow
icefall on the right for two long pitches to easier ground.

North Buttress   300m   Grade III*
First winter ascent not recorded but for an account of an early ascent
of the route (and several others in this guide) see *Mountaineering in
Scotland* by W.H.Murray. This is the huge buttress to the left of Great
Gully, and right of Crowberry Gully. From the foot of Great Gully
two alternatives are possible, the first aims straight up easy ground
for the line of chimneys splitting the middle section of the buttress.
After 130m these lead onto easier angled slopes with the odd difficult
step. An easier approach is to continue along the path past the Water
Slide and climb the lower reaches of Crowberry Gully to the Basin.
From here traverse rightwards to join the chimneys of the first
approach.

North East Zig-Zag   100m   Grade III*
J.R.Marshall, A.H.Hendry and G.J.Ritchie   1957
An interesting climb in open surroundings which has many variations
and is clear of the avalanche problems in Crowberry Gully. Start from
the left end of a broad terrace above and right of Crowberry Gully.
Move up left and then back right by the simplest line to gain the upper
section of North Buttress.

√ Crowberry Gully   300m   Grade III/IV***
H.Raeburn, W.A.Brigg and H.S.Tucker   April 1909
A magnificent classic climb of considerably quality. Unfortunately it

is not often in good condition and can be dangerous due to avalanches. Conditions vary remarkably and can change in a short space of time. It may be completely banked up with snow except for an ice pitch at the junction (where a rightwards rising traverse is made from the foot of the deep recessed Left Fork) and another pitch at the exit from a cave near the top of the gully. The cave will usually give the crux of the normal route (although the Junction pitch can also be quite hard) climbed by the right wall which is invariably of green ice and 10/15m in height. If attempted when out of condition (particularly early in the season) there could be many more pitches and Junction and Cave pitches may be all but impossible with only a thin veneer of verglass.

Crowberry Gully, Left Fork   Grade IV
R.J.Taunton and I.C.Robertson   18th March 1949

The Left Fork leads steeply out of the main gully to the Crowberry Tower Gap. The deeply recessed gully soon becomes a narrow iced chimney which is capped by a large overhanging block. The capstone will always be difficult but good protection is available. Although it is a hard technical problem, this fork is very short and shouldn't require as much time as a complete ascent by the normal route. (Rarely climbed). On the first ascent, a third member of the party could not be pulled over the capstone after the second man had stood on his head to gain elevation!!

Shelf Route   170m   Grade IV**
W.M.MacKenzie and W.H.Murray   March 1937

A superb and sustained climb if good conditions are present. A shallow chimney line running up the left wall of Crowberry Gully. Start low down in Crowberry Gully and traverse left to foot of three chimneys. Climb the right wall and rib of the middle chimney to a shallow trough above. Follow the scoop above between the steep left wall and a small pinnacle. Possible escapes over iced slabs to the ridge on the left. The direct line continues to a recess under the pinnacle from where an awkward right traverse is made to gain icy grooves which lead up to the ridge below Crowberry Tower. Either climb the tower direct and descend its right side to the col (Crowberry Gap) or traverse left towards the top of Curved Ridge.

Crowberry Ridge (Naismith's Original Route)   200m   Grade III**
From the narrows at the foot of Crowberry Gully proper move up
onto the obvious Pinnacle Ledge at the foot of three chimneys. The
left-hand chimney is followed.

Climb up to the right and as soon as possible take the easiest line
back left to the crest. Continue up the crest with easing difficultly to
the Crowberry Tower.

✓ **Curved Ridge/Easy Gully**   300m   Grade II*** (but can attain
Grade III after heavy snowfall)
G.T.Glover and R.G.Napier   April 1898
A magnificent route to the summit of the mountain, it passes through
grand rock scenery, is a good general viewpoint and gives interesting
climbing under almost any conditions. Certainly the most useful
winter climb on the Buachaille and can be quite hard. The line follows
the crest of the ridge throughout. Easier options are available in the
gully to the right of the crest (beware of avalanches).

Climb slightly left out of the Crowberry Basin by any of the several
variations and pass beneath the Rannoch Wall of Crowberry Ridge
(two short steep pitches) to reach a final big cairn, at the top of Curved
Ridge proper and below the foot of Crowberry Tower. From the cairn
a horizontal left traverse for about 30m brings one onto a snow slope
with two gully exits.

1. The gully slanting back to the right reaches the Crowberry Tower
   Gap and from there a short groove leads left then right to the top
   of Crowberry Gully and the final summit slopes.

2. The gully going up slightly leftward leads directly to the summit
   rocks. It is probably the quickest but not the most interesting way.

If time permits, an ascent of the Crowberry Tower can be included if
the first route is followed; from the gap a short corner is climbed to
a ledge on the left then an easy rising spiral traverse leads to the top.
There are more interesting routes up the Tower but this is the easiest
and best in descent.

D Gully   150m   Grade II
G.T.Glover and Collinson   April 1898
The gully below and to the left of Curved Ridge. Usually easy but can give
several short pitches. At the top traverse up and right to Curved Ridge.

D Gully Buttress   150m   Grade III

The buttress is narrow and defined by the deep D Gully on the right and on the left by indefinite rocks merging with Central Buttress with which it forms a right-angle. The start of the buttress is vague and entry is usually made from the foot of D Gully. A prominent steep smooth step high up the buttress is a useful landmark. The first section is fairly easy but then the way is blocked by the steep smooth step. Turn on the left by a shallow chimney and gully leading back rightwards to regain the crest, very narrow at this point. Above, a long slabby section gives the crux, usually climbed near its right edge. After a further 30m or so the buttress ends on a shoulder whence a right traverse should be made to gain Curved Ridge and Easy Gully.

CLIMBS ON STOB DEARG FROM GLEN ETIVE

The Chasm   450m   Grade III/IV

This route is approached from the Glen Etive road (GR 233531), 2½kms from the main road junction. At this point two streams can be seen on the map joining by the road, and The Chasm drains into the northmost one. It forms an obvious gulch on the hillside to the right (west), and is blessed with a short approach. During winters of heavy snowfall this climb may be straightforward. In leaner conditions several pitches will be present and the nature of the climb becomes hard and time-consuming. Several variations exist higher up the gully with the direct continuation being the most difficult. Escapes from the gully can be made at a number of points, most easily to the left.

Lady's Gully   240m   Grade IV

J.R.Marshall, I.D.Haig and G.J.Ritchie (Left Fork)
L.S.Lovat and W.J.R.Greaves (Right Fork)

Easily seen on the hillside to the west of stream junction (GR 240537), this gully is the first one north of The Chasm. Not often in good condition, but when it is (during winters of heavy snowfall and good build-up), the climbing is very good. Follow the line of the gully to a steep wall (45m). Climb the wall, which can be difficult (45m), and several more difficult pitches to a fork in the gully. The left fork is the best option. This leads to easier ground beneath the summit.

THE AONACH EAGACH RIDGE

The Aonach Eagach is the long notched ridge which bounds Glencoe to the north applying particularly to the narrow crest extending between Sgor nam Fionnaidh on the west to Am Bodach at the east end. The Glencoe flank of this ridge is steep and complex, very rocky and seamed by many gullies.

The Aonach Eagach Traverse   3kms end to end   Grade II/III***
In good weather and good conditions the ridge gives a very fine winter expedition. Speed is essential if the party is to avoid an all too frequent benightment. The normal route is from east to west which gives one the advantage of 100m less to climb. Best starting point is from near the white cottage at Allt-na-Reigh. Parking available just down the road (GR 173567). A track leads up, crossing the stream, into the corrie to the east of Am Bodach whence easy slopes lead leftwards to the top (943m). Alternatively one may continue directly up the ridge from the start. Not advised in descent.

The descent from Am Bodach to the west can be quite difficult: go slightly right then back left and down a gully-crack. The most interesting section of the ridge is between Meall Dearg (953m) and Stob Coire Leith (940m), particularly a very narrow pinnacled section and an awkward slabby descent beyond it.

It must be pointed out that there is no safe descent from the ridge on the Glencoe flank between the two end peaks. It is best to continue to the end of the ridge and descend from Sgor nam Fionnaidh to the saddle between it and the Pap of Glencoe. With care it may be possible to descend towards Loch Leven in a northerly direction at a number of points along the ridge.

OUTLYING CLIMBS IN GLENCOE

A'CHAILLACH S.E. FACE

Red Funnel Gully   200m   Grade I/II
R.Baillie, H.MacInnes and party   1964
Interesting for an easy day after heavy snow. It overlooks the road
through the gorge at the top of the Glen on the Aonach Eagach side
and follows the left fork of the steepest gully.

GLEN ETIVE

Dalness Chasm   400m   Grade IV***
H.MacInnes and C.Williamson   February 1979
This obvious watercourse lies opposite the first cottage down Glen
Etive, some 6¹/₂kms from the main road. A tremendous climb, though
rarely in condition. Follow the main stream line with one big pitch
until the triple fork is reached. Take the right fork by steep, short
pitches.

BEINN TRILLEACHAN - ETIVE SLABS
(GS 0944 - Sheet 50 -1:50,000 O.S. Map)
After several days of hard frost water smears running down the slabs
begin to freeze. Two climbs have been made. The first follows an ice
smear near the right side of the main slabs and then tackles roofs and
mixed ground above. The second Dan, Grade IV, takes a much
thicker line of ice up the subsidiary buttress just up and to the right
of the main slabs. Worth a look for a short day.

SRON NA LAIRIG   300m   Grade I/II*
A prominent rocky spur overlooking the head of Lairig Eilde and
leading up onto the south-east ridge of Stob Coire Sgreamhach. The
approach up the Lairig is quite long but gentle. The lower part is best

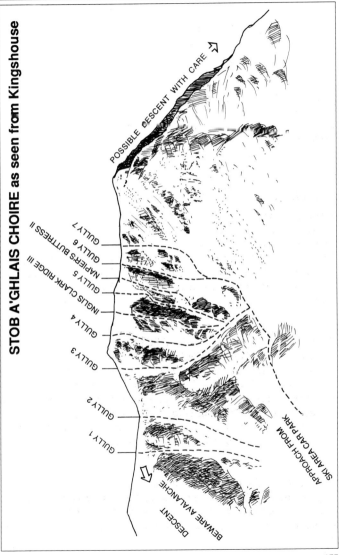

STOB A'GHLAIS CHOIRE as seen from Kingshouse

POSSIBLE DESCENT WITH CARE

GULLY 7
GULLY 6
NAPIERS BUTTRESS II
GULLY 5
INGLIS CLARK RIDGE III
GULLY 4
GULLY 3
GULLY 2
GULLY 1

APPROACH FROM SKI AREA CAR PARK

BEWARE AVALANCHE

DESCENT

avoided on the left, but higher up it narrows to a fine crest. A good primer for the Aonach Eagach.

SGOR NA H-ULAIDH   994m   (GR 111518)

This fine but remote peak lies to the west of Bidean and has several easy climbs on the north face of the mountain. The conspicuous, deep gully directly below the summit gives three or four good pitches and is called Red Gully - Grade III.

N.B. This is a difficult mountain to descend from in poor visibility.

STOB A'GHLAIS CHOIRE   996m   (GR 240516)

Well seen from the Kingshouse the N.E. Face of this mountain appears to be seamed with steep gullies and ridges. On closer inspection the angle relents. However, the routes are all worthwhile for climbers searching for easier ascents away from the crowds. Access is governed by the amount of water in the River Etive. When the river is low it is possible to cross at a number of spots, either before or after Coupall Bridge (GR 243543). A more certain way of avoiding wet feet is to park on the ski road (GR 266525) and skirt the foot of Creag Dhubh. Allow 1½ hours for either approach. In descent the corrie S.E. of the summit of Stob a'Ghlais Choire can be taken. Care should be exercised on these slopes after strong winds or snowfalls, as wind slab avalanches may be present. A longer but more satisfying end to a climb would involve ascending both Creise, 1,110m (GR 238507) and Meall a'Bhuiridh, 1,108m (GR 251503). A descent could then be made through the ski area to the north.

The nature of all the gullies will vary depending on the amount of snow build-up. They will all be easy, Grade I or II. The ridges which separate the gullies are worthy of inspection and will provide steeper mixed climbing at Grade II/III. Also the right-hand skyline will provide an interesting route of ascent, with more difficulty nearer the top. Of particular interest to the climber is the following route:

Inglis Clark Ridge   140m   Grade III*
R.Napier and S.Downie   March 1987

In the centre of the N.E. Face is a broad V-shaped buttress just left of No.5 Gully, the top of which is a flat-topped tower. Start at the right-hand end of the ridge, 30m up No.5 Gully. Follow grooves and some steep ice pitches (crux) to a broad terrace (35m). Ascend to the rock tower and climb it on the right to a wall (65m). Traverse left (5m) along the wall and then up right by blocks and a right-angled corner chimney to the top of the tower.

CICERONE GUIDES

Cicerone publish a wide range of reliable guides to walking and climbing in Europe

FRANCE
TOUR OF MONT BLANC
CHAMONIX MONT BLANC - A Walking Guide
TOUR OF THE OISANS: GR54
WALKING THE FRENCH ALPS: GR5
THE CORSICAN HIGH LEVEL ROUTE: GR20
THE WAY OF ST JAMES: GR65
THE PYRENEAN TRAIL: GR10
TOUR OF THE QUEYRAS
ROCK CLIMBS IN THE VERDON

FRANCE / SPAIN
WALKS AND CLIMBS IN THE PYRENEES
ROCK CLIMBS IN THE PYRENEES

SPAIN
WALKS & CLIMBS IN THE PICOS DE EUROPA
WALKING IN MALLORCA
BIRDWATCHING IN MALLORCA
COSTA BLANCA CLIMBS

FRANCE / SWITZERLAND
THE JURA - Walking the High Route and
  Winter Ski Traverses

SWITZERLAND
WALKS IN THE ENGADINE
THE VALAIS - A Walking Guide
THE ALPINE PASS ROUTE

GERMANY / AUSTRIA
THE KALKALPEN TRAVERSE
KLETTERSTEIG - Scrambles
WALKING IN THE BLACK FOREST
MOUNTAIN WALKING IN AUSTRIA
WALKING IN THE SALZKAMMERGUT
KING LUDWIG WAY

ITALY
ALTA VIA - High Level Walkis in the Dolomites
VIA FERRATA - Scrambles in the Dolomites
ITALIAN ROCK - Selected Rock Climbs in
  Northern Italy
CLASSIC CLIMBS IN THE DOLOMITES

OTHER AREAS
THE MOUNTAINS OF GREECE - A Walker's
  Guide
CRETE: Off the beaten track
Treks & Climbs in the mountains of RHUM &
PETRA, JORDAN
THE ATLAS MOUNTAINS

GENERAL OUTDOOR BOOKS
LANDSCAPE PHOTOGRAPHY
FIRST AID FOR HILLWALKERS
MOUNTAIN WEATHER
MOUNTAINEERING LITERATURE
SKI THE NORDIC WAY
THE ADVENTURE ALTERNATIVE

CANOEING
SNOWDONIA WILD WATER, SEA & SURF
WILDWATER CANOEING
A CANOEIST'S GUIDE TO NORTHERN
  ENGLAND (East)

CARTOON BOOKS
ON FOOT & FINGER
ON MORE FEET & FINGERS
LAUGHS ALONG THE PENNINE WAY

*Also a full range of guidebooks
to walking, scrambling, ice-climbing,
rock climbing, and other adventurous
pursuits in Britain and abroad*

CICERONE

Other guides are constantly being added to the Cicerone List.
Available from bookshops, outdoor equipment shops or direct (send for price list)
from CICERONE, 2 POLICE SQUARE, MILNTHORPE, CUMBRIA, LA7 7PY

Printed in Gt. Britain by
CARNMOR PRINT & DESIGN
95-97 LONDON RD. PRESTON

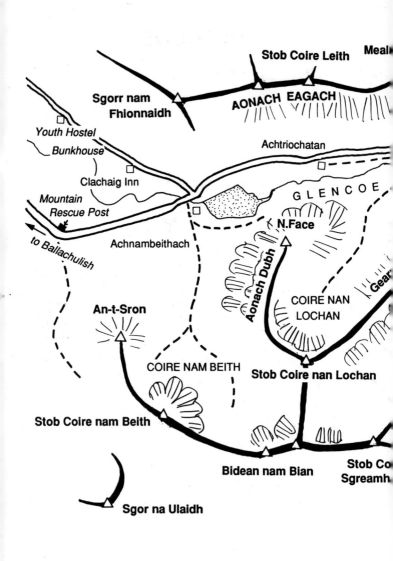